Southern Literary Studies
Louis D. Rubin, Jr., Editor

On the Prejudices, Predilections, and Firm Beliefs of William Faulkner

On the Prejudices, Predilections, and Firm Beliefs of William Faulkner

ESSAYS BY
CLEANTH BROOKS

LOUISIANA STATE UNIVERSITY PRESS
BATON ROUGE AND LONDON

Copyright © 1987 by Louisiana State University Press
All rights reserved
Manufactured in the United States of America
Designer: Sylvia Malik Loftin
Typeface: Galliard
Typesetter: G & S Typesetters, Inc.
Printer: Thomson-Shore, Inc.
Binder: John H. Dekker & Sons, Inc.

10 9 8 7 6 5 4 3 2 1

Library of Congress Cataloging-in-Publication Data

Brooks, Cleanth, 1906–
    On the prejudices, predilections, and firm beliefs
of William Faulkner.

    (Southern literary studies)
    Includes bibliographical references and index.
    1. Faulkner, William, 1897–1962—Criticism and
interpretation.   I. Title.   II. Series.
PS3511.A86Z6384   1987   813'.52   87-2968
ISBN 0-8071-1391-3

To

Albert Russel Erskine

A great editor and a true man of letters

Contents

Preface

The dates of composition of these essays span fifteen years—from 1971 to 1985. They represent further speculations on Faulkner and his works made well after my having completed *William Faulkner: The Yoknapatawpha Country*. A number of them were written to answer questions such as What did Faulkner really believe? Was or was not Gavin Stevens his mouthpiece? Did Faulkner believe in progress? What was his attitude toward the poor whites of the South?

I believe that answers to such questions were at least implied in my studies of the novels and the short stories. But an essay rather specifically focused upon the question allows for more explicit answers. The essay form also makes it easier to provide a rebuttal to some of the allegations made about Faulkner or with reference to him by scholars who are customarily more careful and more properly attentive to the evidence.

I have not included all the special essays that I have written about Faulkner. Some repeat or say, I believe, less well, what is contained in one or another of the essays in the present collection. In general I have tried to avoid too much overlapping with my previous books on Faulkner, though some overlapping is inevitable—a man doesn't change his convictions from year to year simply to be sure of presenting something fresh.

My hope in reissuing these essays is that they will come at typical Faulknerian topics from a new angle or make use of a new focus and so justify their inclusion here.

On the Prejudices, Predilections, and Firm Beliefs of William Faulkner

Faulkner
and the
Fugitive-Agrarians

The two most brilliant manifestations of the great upsurge of letters in the twentieth-century South were the advent of William Faulkner, of Oxford, Mississippi, and of the Fugitive poets of Nashville, Tennessee. These events were not interconnected, but they did occur at about the same time. Faulkner's first volume, *The Marble Faun,* a long poem, was published in 1924. Several of his novels rapidly followed: *Soldiers' Pay,* in 1926; *Mosquitoes,* in 1927; and *Sartoris* and *The Sound and the Fury,* both in 1929. It was *The Sound and the Fury* that made a resounding impact. It is, of course, as a powerful novelist, not as a poet, that Faulkner is known today. The Fugitives also began as poets, and though some of them were to become novelists, they are still best known for their poetry, which appeared in their own publication, the *Fugitive* (1922—1925), and elsewhere. But in 1930 a number of these poets joined other friends in publishing *I'll Take My Stand.* This Agrarian manifesto was a collection of twelve essays on Southern culture in its various aspects. It was praised as a defense of Southern values or, and more usually, condemned as the work of a group of unreconstructed Confederates. So the Fugitive-Agrarians made their impact in a dual capacity—as writers of a rather quirky intellectual poetry and as conservative critics of the culture. But one notes that the dates of their

Given as a lecture at the 1981 Faulkner Conference at Oxford, Miss., and originally published in slightly different form in *Faulkner and the Southern Renaissance* (Jackson, 1982).

appearance on the literary scene and of Faulkner's almost exactly coincide.

There is little evidence that the Fugitives took any notice of Faulkner's poetry or he of theirs. Actually they had on this level almost nothing in common. The Fugitives were in conscious rebellion against Swinburne, Dowson, and the early Yeats. They were defiantly experimental. On the other hand, Faulkner's poetry was redolent of the Victorians and of the British decadents of the 1890s. But when it came to Faulkner's novels, the Fugitive camp was quick to notice and to respond.

This latter point is one worth making and fully developing in view of the fact that the relations between these two manifestations of the new Southern literature have heretofore been so little explored as to give rise to misconceptions. Hints of rivalry have got about, particularly the notion that the Nashville poets were reluctant to recognize talent outside their own snug little circle, and that only after the acclaim of Faulkner's achievement had become a tidal wave did they join in praise for him. What had amounted to no more than a hint or suspicion of such jealous coolness was put quite clearly and emphatically in 1973 by Daniel Aaron in his book entitled *The Unwritten War: American Writers and the Civil War*. Aaron begins his chapter on William Faulkner as follows:

> Only after the flurry of Agrarianism petered out did the Neo-Confederates come to a proper appreciation of William Faulkner. Some of them knew him, of course, in the 1930s as one of the talented representatives of the Southern literary "renaissance," but a decade passed before they canonized him belatedly as "the most powerful and original novelist in the United States" and as "one of the best in the modern world," and inadvertently made his achievement ancillary to their own social and aesthetic dicta. The exegesis of Warren and especially of Cleanth Brooks influenced Faulkner scholarship so profoundly, in fact, that the differences between him and the Nashville group have become obscured. Yet Faulkner remained outside the Agrarian orbit.

The rather dubious compliment paid to the power of my influence is not supported by the facts of the case. Indeed, the entire argument set forth in the paragraph from which I have quoted will not bear inspection. It is just not grounded in fact. Professor Aaron's so-called Neo-

Confederates were not an organized agit-prop group, a kind of Chinese tong equipped with hatchet men. They were a group of friends who shared some common views, but had their own firmly maintained opinions. A glance through the letters of Davidson and Tate, for example, will make abundantly clear how frequently they disagreed with each other.

A further fact needs clearing up. They did not write *I'll Take My Stand* in the hope of becoming a force in political affairs and then, when the ploy failed to catch on, proceed to take up *belles lettres* as a means to fame and fortune. Yet is this not what Aaron suggests? If not, his first sentence involves a complete non sequitur. For what otherwise is the logical connection between a failure at effective sectional polemic and a belated proper "appreciation" of William Faulkner? Actually, the most overtly polemical of all the Agrarians, Donald Davidson, was very quick to appreciate Faulkner and give his work high praise.

Consider once more the passage quoted by Aaron, that in which someone refers to Faulkner as the most powerful and original novelist in the United States and one of the best in the modern world. The person who wrote that was Allen Tate. Aaron quotes it from an essay that Tate published in 1945. Now in 1945, Faulkner still had no nationwide popularity. I can testify to that personally, for when I first began to teach Faulkner at Yale in the autumn of 1947 there were only two volumes by Faulkner in print and both were cheap Modern Library editions. I searched the secondhand bookshops for copies of such masterpieces as *Light in August, Absalom, Absalom!, The Hamlet,* and *Go Down, Moses* in order to find extra texts. Faulkner became known nationally only after he had been awarded the Nobel Prize in 1950. There were individual critics who praised him before that date, and the Fugitive-Agrarians were among that band of critics. Let us examine the facts.

In 1926, Donald Davidson promptly reviewed *Soldiers' Pay* on his book page in the Nashville *Tennessean*. It was a favorable notice, and he declared that Faulkner wrote better than either Dos Passos or Sinclair Lewis. In the next year, 1927, Davidson reviewed *Mosquitoes*. He had some reservations about this work, which most of us consider Faulkner's weakest, but he was "full of admiration" for what he called Faulkner's performance in it and observed that Faulkner had by now happily assimilated Joyce. In 1929, Davidson reviewed *Sartoris*, Faulkner's third novel, and wrote that "as a stylist and as an acute observer of human behavior . . . Mr. Faulkner is the equal of any except three or four American novelists who stand at the very top." Further on in his review Davidson remarked that Faulkner "needs only to find a theme worthy of his talent and perception." This prophecy was, of course, soon to be fulfilled, for Faulkner's masterpieces began to appear almost at once. In 1935, when *Publishers Weekly* asked Davidson as a Southerner and as a by-this-time well known book reviewer to name the best Southern novels of the past and the present, he included two by Faulkner: *The Sound and the Fury* (1929) and *As I Lay Dying* (1930).

R. P. Warren has told me that he read Faulkner's first novel in 1929. This was the year in which the English edition first appeared. (Warren was then in his second year at Oxford. I was also at Oxford at the time, and read the English edition.) In 1931, Warren was praising Faulkner to his faculty associates, as Blotner has recorded, and in that same year Warren reviewed, and favorably, Faulkner's first collection of short stories, *These Thirteen*. Warren has gone on through his own literary career to write intelligently and sensitively about Faulkner's work. But for the moment I am concerned to establish a more immediate point: that the Fugitive-Agrarians, from a very early date, were aware of, and on record about, Faulkner's promise and his genius.

With John Crowe Ransom, the response to Faulkner's work was somewhat mixed. When Ransom reviewed *Pylon* in March of 1935 the title of the review read: "Faulkner: South's Most Brilliant But Wayward Talent, Is Spent." Yet a month later, in an essay in the *Virginia Quarterly Review,* Ransom called Faulkner "the most exciting figure in our contemporary literature." And Warren has told me of a conversation that he and Ransom had about Faulkner in the spring of that same year in which Ransom explained that though he didn't like *Pylon,* he admired most of Faulkner's work immensely. Later, in 1945, while Ransom was editing the *Kenyon Review,* he joined enthusiastically in plans for a number of the *Kenyon* to be given over exclusively to Faulkner criticism. Unfortunately, the plans fell through when a sufficient number of articles on Faulkner were not forthcoming. (How changed this situation is today: we have, I expect, too many people writing about Faulkner. An editor who planned a Faulkner number today would be virtually overrun by would-be contributors.)

A fourth Fugitive, Allen Tate, apparently did not review any of Faulkner's early novels, though there is no reason to suppose that he was not aware of a man whom his friends had been praising for some years. The Davidson-Tate correspondence makes reference to Faulkner as early as 1932.

The best refutation to the implication that people such as Allen Tate did not climb aboard the Faulkner bandwagon until it had got up momentum lies in the character and personality of Allen Tate. He was all his life scornful of such intellectual acrobatics. He held himself aloof from literary self-promotion of every sort. As a critic, he was the least impressionistic, the least impulsive, of all that this country has produced. He took a pride in informed and reasoned judgments. One may disagree on occasion with his judgments, or with the reasons adduced for proposing them, but one could be sure that they were never thoughtless or self-serving in their motivation.

Tate's final appraisal of Faulkner (in 1963) as one of the best writers in the modern world went hand in hand with a personal dislike for Faulkner, a dislike which he freely acknowledged. I shall not try to justify Tate's personal dislike for Faulkner, though I can understand it. Faulkner was essentially a shy man, and his modesty in part accounts for his being uncomfortable with university professors, writers of national renown, and representatives of the press. Part of his self-deprecation was his unwillingness to call himself a literary man. He was, he said, simply a teller of tales or, even more simply, just a farmer. Such downplaying of the role of the artist irritated Tate, who set great store by the vocation of poet and novelist, and liked to point to the veneration in which the French, for example, held their men of letters, compared to the disparagement offered them in the United States in the thirties and forties.

In any case, Faulkner was not easy to get to know. I remember a story that the late Thornton Wilder told me. He admired Faulkner's work very much and looked forward to meeting him in Boston and talking to him about his play, *Requiem for a Nun,* which was just opening there. Had I, at that time, known Wilder much better, I would have told him: don't try to get him into literary conversation right off. You'll scare him to death. He probably is already overawed by your reputation. A highly successful dramatist who is also a learned man will cause him to shrink into a corner. But I could not tell Wilder this—at that time we barely knew each other—and sure enough, as Wilder ruefully told me later, the worst had happened. Faulkner had withdrawn into himself. No rapport was established. Wilder was disappointed and perhaps his feelings were hurt. But the story has a happy ending, for later the two men met again. Somehow this time they did hit it off and Faulkner became warm and friendly.

I mention Tate's personal dislike for Faulkner—and there was, I would assume, an answering dislike in Faulkner for him—simply to make an important point. Tate's high praise of Faulkner's work was in the best sense disinterested. In proclaiming Faulkner one of the great writers of the century, he was neither climbing onto a bandwagon nor influenced by his regard for a friend. His praise reflected his considered opinion.

To make the tally complete, I ought to say a word here about Andrew Lytle, the novelist and Agrarian. On the subject of Faulkner I find nothing by him in print in the early period, but he has published three fine essays on Faulkner, generous in praise and highly perceptive, particularly in regard to Faulkner's account of the individual in his relation to society and specifically to the older Southern society.

Now we must return once more to Professor Aaron's account of the relation between the Fugitive-Agrarians and Faulkner. Aaron's reason for praising Faulkner and disparaging the Nashville group amounts to this: The latter group were extremist Neo-Confederates, indulging in special pleading for their section, intransigent secessionists still, whereas Faulkner was able to stand back from the more emotional issues, regard the faults of the older Southern culture with a critical eye, and thus achieve a mature fiction, one that accorded with the facts of history and with universal humanistic values. In the interests of brevity, I have paraphrased and condensed Aaron's full argument, but I believe that I am giving a fair account of what it is. Without arguing the matter of whether or not the South had real grievances that ought to have been redressed, and that, in spite of black chattel slavery, the Old South possessed certain virtues, I think that I can meet Aaron on his chosen ground.

What Aaron does is to measure Faulkner's later and more detached work against the most intemperate and intransigent writings—mostly early—of the Nashville group. Had he taken account of Faulkner's early novels he would have found Faulkner about as unreconstructed as anybody, with at least a measure of glorification of romantic Confederate cavalrymen, and even with some stereotypes of the contented slave. Irving Howe, for example, has reproached him for such. Similar indictments by Northern critics were made right on down to *Intruder in the Dust* (1949). On the other hand, one can find plenty of detachment, soul-searching, and critical self-examination in the writings of Ransom, Warren, and Tate. Only Davidson and Lytle might be deemed partial exceptions.

In *The Fathers* (1938), for example, Tate provides an account of the Virginia patriarch whose life is thoroughly ordered by tradition. As Tate describes it, the tradition is out of touch with reality, and Major Buchan, the patriarch, acts so rigidly in accordance with it that he actually disowns his son. Tate's attitude is "mature" indeed: if the older order has virtues, it also has major deficiencies and defects. Aaron acknowledges as much in his specific discussion of *The Fathers,* but in his summary of the Fugitive-Agrarians' relationship to Faulkner he scarcely takes it into account. In fact, as I look back over the writings of the Fugitive-Agrarians I find very little that simplistically defends the Old South. The poetry of Ransom, Tate, and Warren is very mature indeed—some will call it almost sternly intellectual. The same can be said of Warren's fiction. It reflects no idyllic legend of the Old South, though one ought also to point out that neither are Warren and Tate taken in by the American Dream. That dream is indeed present in their various writings, but only as a promise yet to be fulfilled.

In short, it would be a fair procedure to compare the myth of the Old South with the myth of the New America, or to compare the realities of the Old Southern culture with the realities of the civilization of the North. But to demolish one myth by pointing out that it was mythical—not literally fulfilled and real—while at the same time asserting that the other dream was no dream but a matter of fact, is neither fair reporting nor good history. Specifically, "America the Beautiful," one has ruefully to admit, is still mostly a dream. America's "alabaster cities" *have* been "dimmed by human tears." Her purple mountain majesties overshadow an Appalachia with a population which have lived for centuries in dire poverty. The American Dream is a noble one, but it is not to be taken as an accurate reflection of our lived experience.

Aaron's special praise for Faulkner was that he grew out of a defensive parochialism into a detached and rather dispassionate judgment of his native region. Such a view seems to me substantially correct and represents a fair appraisal of Faulkner's achievement. But ironically for Aaron's estimate of the essential difference between Faulkner and, say, Tate or Warren or Ransom, the very best single statement of the necessity for Southern self-criticism was penned by Allen Tate. In his fine 1959 essay, "A Southern Mode of the Imagination," Tate provided the very basis for Aaron's own 1973 approval of Faulkner: that is to say, Tate pointed out that Faulkner and even lesser members of the Southern Renaissance were at last able to look at their native region from a distance—to move from defensiveness to intelligent criticism, to come to realize that everything wrong with the South, as Tate puts it in a memorable phrase, "could not be blamed on the Yankees." Nevertheless, Tate continued to think that the Yankees were blameworthy in some important regards. Or to put matters more positively, he found certain virtues in the Southern tradition that he regarded as worth defending and preserving. And so did Faulkner.

I've spent a considerable time on what the Nashville group thought about Faulkner. What did he think about them? I simply don't know. There seems to be very little in print on the subject. Among his *Selected Letters* (1977) there is a passage of high praise of the Cass Mastern episode in Warren's *All the King's Men*, though he wrote rather disparagingly of the novel as a whole. Perhaps someone will come to tell us from memory what Faulkner said about this or that one of the group. But in print thus far I have found only one further scrap of evidence and it comes not from a Faulkner letter or interview but from a speech that Faulkner puts into the mouth of one of his characters. In "Knight's Gambit" (1940) Charles Mallison observes to himself that "Huey Long in Louisiana had made himself founder owner and supporter of what his uncle Gavin said was one of the best literary magazines anywhere, without ever once looking inside it." I would like to think that Gavin Stevens was here speaking for Faulkner himself. In 1935 we had invited Faulkner to a writers' conference that was to be held in Baton Rouge that spring, the conference at which the foundation of the *Southern Review* was announced. We got from Faulkner a polite refusal couched in the most modest terms possible. For he wrote that he would have liked to come but had nothing to contribute. Later, Warren and I tried to get a story from him for the *Review,* but we were aware that such a catch was unlikely. We could pay only one and a half cents a word, and Faulkner needed the best payment he could get—the rate paid by the *Saturday Evening Post* and such—to meet his household expenses during the years when his great novels were being written but did not sell. Whether or not Gavin Stevens's high opinion of the *Southern Review* was shared by Faulkner himself, his guess that Long never looked inside its covers is a shrewd one. I myself doubt that Long ever knew the *Review* existed. He was dead before the second issue appeared.

If the relation of Faulkner to the Fugitive-Agrarians has now been cleared up—and the available evidence seems to support my conclusion—what remains to be said on this general subject? Two things in particular, I should think. First, what did Faulkner lose—or perhaps gain—by being a kind of literary "loner"? And second, what interests, beliefs, and attitudes did Faulkner and the Fugitives have in common? I am going to deny, of course, that the exegeses of his work done by Warren and by me were designed to make it appear that he shared our views. In any case, Faulkner was too big to be attracted into anybody else's orbit. Warren and I would have been fools to think so.

With regard to the first question, I think that I can be rather brief. Many writers have found that a fairly close-knit literary fellowship is a positive aid toward producing good literature. There was such a literary group in the golden age of the literature of New England, for example, but even at that time and in that place there was a Melville, who seems not to have had or needed close literary affiliations. The truth is that almost any literary situation might conceivably provide sufficient nourishment for the production of good and even great literary art. Some personalities seem to prefer relative solitude, others a congenial group of friends. In any case, the presence of a literary community will not make up for a lack of talent. As someone observed long ago, good poems are not written by committees, nor are good novels. In an important sense, every writer is self-taught—has to find his own mode of utterance and devise his own language. The Fugitive poets, for example, showed no standard pattern—did not conform in the least to a house style. In fact, the major poets of this group are so diverse in the ways of saying something that one could never for a moment confuse a poem by Davidson with one by Tate, or a poem by Warren with one by Ransom.

Of course, to have the association of a group of friendly critics who know you well and share your literary interests does confer great benefits. In some comments published in the *Harvard Advocate* (1951), Ransom draws upon his experience with his fellow Fugitives as he comments on Faulkner. He observes that Faulkner had "not had the advantage of the society of his literary peers" or that of "intellectuals with their formidable dialectic." I agree. Every careful reader of Faulkner can see that this lack shows up in numerous small ways. Like Humpty-Dumpty, Faulkner sometimes made particular words mean what he wanted them to mean—the dictionary be hanged. Yet in the same passage Ransom sets out some of the advantages of Faulkner's relative isolation—which was, of course, never absolute: from the beginning there were Phil Stone and Ben Wasson to talk matters over with. Ransom remarks that for Faulkner there was no acquaintance with the literary "academy [to] adulterate the natural directness of his style." Ransom sums up with a resounding compliment. He writes that Faulkner's "perfections are wonderful and well sustained, and without exact precedent anywhere." In short, the leader of the Fugitives could see certain advantages that Faulkner had in not being a member of any literary group.

The second point—and the more important one, of course—is this: What did Faulkner and the Fugitives have in common, if anything? Did they see their native region in much the same way? I've earlier indicated that they did, but we need some illustrations. In spite of their rather different approaches to poetry, they were equally concerned to explore what was good in the Southern tradition and to fortify and preserve it. They did not oppose change, but they saw that change was not in itself necessarily good and that sudden drastic changes could be disastrous for a culture. Neither, by the way, looked uncritically at the plantation system too often tied to a one-crop economy. The Fugitive-Agrarians stressed a mixed economy, including mixed farming conducted basically by yeoman farmers. This bias in part reflected the situation in the upper South, the subregion from which most of the Agrarians came. But since Faulkner also was well aware of the perils of the slave system on which the great plantations depended, he hardly differed on this point from the Fugitives. In what high regard Faulkner held the yeoman farmers of his own state comes clear in his fiction. Although he wrote some of his most powerful novels about the founding of the great plantations and about the later generations of such planter stock, he had a genuine respect for the small farmer, and his characters like the McCallums or V. K. Ratliff possess backbone and determination and also moral force. We make a grave mistake if we take as representative of this class of yeoman farmer the despicable Anse Bundren or the ridiculous I. O. Snopes.

To turn to the Fugitives once more. In Donald Davidson's fine essay "Still Rebels, Still Yankees," the heroes are small farmers from Georgia who live what Davidson sees as a good life, unpretentious and quiet though it be. They are still rebels against the soulless secularism of modern industrial civilization. But so are the Yankees depicted in his essay, the yeoman farmers of Vermont who have character and the richness and tang of their native background to match those of their Georgia counterparts. Davidson exults in them both. He is delighted with their local differences, which do not for him constitute any denial of their essentially common values. Those who want to convict Davidson of a narrow and intransigent Southern nationalism and of itching to fight the Civil War over again ought to read this essay.

To assess the parallels that exist between Faulkner and the Fugitive-Agrarians, let us have some concrete examples. Although generalizations are important, they need to be defined, illustrated, and generally nailed down by specific illustrations from the poetry and fiction being discussed.

Yet, let me begin with a fairly obvious generalization. With Faulkner, the Fugitives shared a passionate devotion to the land in which they lived and which had brought them forth. For them the various bits of American landscape were not interchangeable parts, each asking for as much or as little love as any other. For Faulkner and the Fugitives, their native landscape was alive with the deeds of men, a region literally steeped in history. One of the closing paragraphs of *Sartoris* (1929) reads in part: "The dusk was peopled with ghosts of glamorous and old disastrous things. And if they were just glamorous enough, there would be a Sartoris in them. . . . For there is death in the sound of [this name], and a glamorous fatality, like silver pennons down rushing at sunset, in a dying fall of horns along the road to Ronsevaux." This is Faulkner's final salute to the family of the Sartorises who gave their name to his third-to-be-published novel. They are a romantic and daredevil breed, and the young Bayard Sartoris whose actions bring this novel to a close is clearly a hero built on the old Byronic model, a hero who is imprudent to the point of sheer folly, but to whom women are powerfully attracted and whose career is indeed glamorous. Faulkner's prose poetry in this passage retains the tonality of romantic verse, filled with echoes of Housman and Swinburne. But Faulkner sees the Sartoris breed, with some warrant, as specifically Southern. The Old South was the kind of world that could produce this kind of man, and the South itself—"peopled with ghosts of glamorous and old disastrous things"—partakes of their quality.

If one turns to John Crowe Ransom on the subject of the South, the tonality of the poetry is clearly different. There are no echoes of the British poetry of the 1890s. The verse is invincibly modern. Yet notice the resemblances. The land described in the poem from which I shall quote is like Faulkner's land, impoverished. Some would even call it too worn out to yield a decent crop. Its great crop is memory and history. As the poet puts it:

> We pluck the spindling ears and gather the corn.
> One spot has special yield? "On this spot stood
> Heroes and drenched it with their only blood."
> And talk meets talk, as echoes from the horn
> Of the hunter—echoes are the old man's arts,
> Ample are the chambers of their hearts.

In the next stanza the hunters come into sight in this autumn landscape. But if this foxhunt reminds us of chivalry—a cavalry charge, say—it is itself little more than a faraway echo. It is play—not a practical activity—for what is pursued is in itself of no value: one doesn't eat foxes—doesn't really want to catch them. The chase is its own reward.

> Here come the hunters, keepers of a rite:
> The horn, the hounds, the lank mares coursing by
> Straddled with archetypes of chivalry;
> And the fox, lovely ritualist in flight
> Offering his unearthly ghost to quarry
> And the fields, themselves to harry.

If such a stanza rather undercuts the value of chivalric glory, the love of the land itself is strongly asserted in the closing stanzas of the poem. Granted that this land is unprosperous, no place for a young man to make his fortune, the young are exhorted not to leave it—for they have a deep emotional allegiance to it. If someone tells them "that easily will your hands / More prosper in other lands,"

> Angry as wasp-music be your cry then:
> "Forsake the Proud Lady, of the heart of fire,
> The look of snow, to the praise of a dwindled choir,
> Song of degenerate specters that were men?
> The sons of the fathers shall keep her, worthy of
> What those have done in love."

The mystique of the South as a kind of sacred land is as unmistakable here as in Faulkner's patch of purple prose. In spite of the taut angularity of Ransom's verse, the attitude is fully as romantic. The South is the Proud Lady, a kind of patron goddess.

The relation of all these writers to their native soil went very deep. I could give dozens of instances from Faulkner and dozens from the poetry and prose of the Fugitive-Agrarians. But for all their depth of emotion, they keep their eyes on the object. They rarely if ever drift into mawkish local patriotism. Faulkner's realism and his sense of humor also tend to keep him free of it, while the Fugitives' tart sense of irony is their special safeguard. Moreover, as I have already suggested, the South is for neither party just a landscape. The scene is so closely related to its history and to the character of its people that the celebration of a landscape for its merely pictorial qualities is rare. This means that one's emotion has to do with a whole complex of relations and one's sense of affiliation is also complex. Several times an author went so far as to speak of his relation to the South as a love-hate relation.

There are many parallels, but a particularly exact one occurs in Faulkner's *Light in August* and Warren's *All the King's Men*. In Warren's novel, the Cass Mastern episode tells of the young Mastern's betrayal of his best friend. Mastern had seduced his friend's beautiful wife, or, as the novel makes plain, it was really the other way around: she had seduced him. Now Mastern was a sensitive and idealistic young man, and when he found out that his friend's sudden death was not accidental as was first thought, but an act of suicide at having discovered his double betrayal by friend and wife, Mastern feels a terrible remorse.

An attractive slave girl in the friend's household, the wife's personal maid, had made the same discovery as Mastern. The unfaithful woman, suspecting this, sells the girl down the river, probably to end up in a New Orleans brothel. When Mastern learns that the slave girl has been sold, he makes frantic efforts to find the new buyer, intending to buy her back and give her her freedom. But this search is fruitless, though his desire to make amends or at least to do penance remains unabated. The Civil War had just broken out, and Mastern found a solution in joining the Confederate army, but as an act of expiation, for he makes a vow to himself that he will never fire a shot at the enemy. In fact, he longs for the enemy bullet that will end his own life. The narrator writes that if Mastern "had put on the gray jacket in anguish of spirit and in hope of expiation, he came to wear it in pride, for it was a jacket like those worn by the men with whom he marched. 'I have seen men do brave things,' Mastern wrote, 'and they ask for nothing.' And he added, 'It is not hard to love men for the things they endure.'" Finally, in the battles around Atlanta, Mastern receives the bullet he had longed for and dies in reconciliation with his God. He writes, "I have lived to do no man good, and have seen others suffer for my sin. I do not question the Justice of God, that others have suffered for my sin, for it may be that only by the suffering of the innocent does God affirm that men are brothers."

No wonder Faulkner admired this tale: it developed a dramatic situation dear to his own heart. But Faulkner's use of the instance of a Confederate soldier's taking part in the defense of his country but refusing to fire at the enemy is only incidental to the two main stories that he narrates in *Light in August*. Near the end of that novel Faulkner tells us about the family background of the Reverend Gail Hightower. His grandfather had been a profane, hard-driving, utterly reckless Confederate cavalryman, but his son, Gail Hightower's father, was a man of an entirely different stripe: a homemade abolitionist, something of a puritan who practiced the restrictive virtues; yet also a brave man who "during the four years" of the war "had never fired a gun."

Did such Southerners exist? Are Faulkner and Warren simply inventing such characters for their own fictional purposes? I think not. We have plenty of proof that Southerners existed who disliked slavery and who opposed secession to the very end, but loyally went into the Southern armies when hostilities commenced. *Mary Chesnut's Civil*

War, so superbly edited by Vann Woodward, provides numerous examples. Both Faulkner and Warren, though they did not claim to be
historians, actually knew their Southern history very well.

Although I have not dealt exhaustively with the parallels between
the fiction of Faulkner and the poetry and fiction of the Nashville
group, perhaps I have adduced enough to drive home my point:
namely, that for all their differences in forms, tonalities, and specific
subject matters, these writers differed very little in their devotion to
their native region and what they have to say about it in praise and in
reproof. I shall not undertake to compare the worth of their various
achievements. In any case, I have no wish to revise the Fugitive Allen
Tate's own praise of Faulkner as the most powerful and original novelist in the United States.

Faulkner's
Ultimate
Values

In the last twenty-five years I have often been asked, What did Faulkner really believe about man and his relation to the universe in which he finds himself? What were Faulkner's ultimate values? What did he think of Christianity? These are perfectly proper questions and I have often asked them of myself. But they are not easy to answer—at least if a rather specific answer is demanded. What makes the problem more difficult is that the answers that Faulkner gave, during the last thirty-odd years of his life, to the various people who interviewed him are usually vague, highly subjective, and frequently contradict each other.

Faulkner said, for example, that he believed in God but had some problems with accepting Christianity. Yet at another time he remarked that Christianity provides the supreme example of compassion and self-sacrifice—two virtues that Faulkner held in the highest esteem. Furthermore, at various times Faulkner did call himself a Christian, though he wanted to define the word in his own terms. The best book that I know on this general subject is by John Hunt. It is entitled *William Faulkner: Art in Theological Tension* (1965). Hunt's conclusion is that though Faulkner veered toward stoicism, he remained, on the whole, rather close to the Christian revelation. I cheerfully accept this estimate. Although Hunt is a layman, he has had solid theological

Given as a lecture at the 1981 Faulkner Conference at Oxford, Miss., and originally published in slightly different form in *Faulkner and the Southern Renaissance* (Jackson, 1982).

training and he has a detailed acquaintance with Faulkner's work. Faulkner's stoicism comes out rather clearly in his stress on endurance. More than one of the characters in his fiction discovers that a man sometimes finds that he can endure almost anything, and Faulkner compels some of his characters to endure a great deal. Think, for instance, of the Tall Convict adrift on the raging floodwaters of the Mississippi. The stoic bias in Faulkner comes out also in his little concern for God's grace—either as a concept or as an experience that is vouchsafed to any of his fictional characters. But Faulkner's own early nurture in Christianity was indeed powerful, and I agree with Hunt in finding a great deal of residual Christianity in his writings—even though that Christianity is rarely, if ever, presented in precise theological terms.

Yet since Faulkner was not versed in theology, and since very few of us are—I certainly make no such pretense for myself—I think that my best method of procedure is to make no further references to what Faulkner at one time or another declared to be his beliefs, but to try to discover his beliefs as they are presented, in dramatic terms, in his fiction. After all, his great accomplishment was in his fiction. There we will find him speaking most truthfully—and least ambiguously—about the values that make meaningful the lives of men and women.

One of Faulkner's most interesting and quasi-theological discussions occurs in *Go Down, Moses*.[1] Isaac McCaslin is engaged in a debate with his elder cousin, McCaslin Edmonds. Their general topic is the nature of man and mankind's characteristic virtues and vices. Isaac asserts that God "had seen in individual cases [that men] were capable of anything any height or depth" (282). And surely young Isaac is correct. Man can rise to heights far above those of any of his fellow creatures, but then again he can also sink to depths below those of any beast. That is to say, unless a human being is better than a mere animal, he or she is bound to be worse than any animal.

Isaac goes on to say that God knew all about men's capacities for both good and evil because He "had created them and knew them capable of all things because He had shaped them out of the primal Absolute which contained all" (292). This version is not precisely the orthodox Christian account of a good creation in complete harmony

---

1. Quotations from Faulkner's novels are from the first editions.

with its maker God, a relation to the Creator which man broke through his own perverse will. Nevertheless, Faulkner is careful to shy away from any notion that man is naturally good, and he avoids the Gnostic heresy which blames the Creator of the universe for placing mankind in an evil world. In sum, Faulkner insists on man's responsibility for his actions. Elsewhere he will stress that point in saying that man must strive to be just a little better than one would normally expect him to be. In short, man's better nature must strive against his worse, and Faulkner clearly believes that there is a better and a worse. It is not sufficient that man should simply do what comes naturally, for man is not naturally good. He is created with a potentiality for good, but he must achieve it—and Faulkner seems to imply that it must be largely through his own efforts.

Later still, Faulkner was to say in his Nobel Prize speech that the great theme of literature is that "of the human heart in conflict with itself." Faulkner's characteristic saints and heroes are those who come out of this conflict as victors over themselves.

Now that I have completed this perhaps overlengthy preamble, let me ask, What are the virtues that Faulkner stresses in his fiction? One can find a convenient, though not necessarily exhaustive, list of them in *Go Down, Moses*. I have already mentioned the long debate between Isaac and his elder cousin. There McCaslin Edmonds tries to define truth for the younger man. Truth—by which of course he means the truth that governs or ought to govern all human actions—"Truth covers all things that touch the heart—honor and pride and pity and justice and courage and love" (297). All the virtues listed come in for great emphasis in Faulkner's fiction, a fact that any reader of his novels can easily corroborate. In what is to follow I mean to give some examples and illustrations from specific passages of the stories and novels. These will show more precisely than any abstract definitions can what Faulkner meant by pride or honor.

Let me begin, then, with courage. For Faulkner, it was apparently the prime virtue. It is indeed a basic, though not necessarily the highest virtue, for courage undergirds all the other virtues. Let me illustrate. In the New Testament we are told that when someone smites you on the cheek, you should turn the other cheek. Yet if you turn the other cheek simply because you are afraid not to, then you have exercised no virtue at all—mere cowardice. To turn the other cheek is only virtuous if you do it not out of fear but, though you have the courage to strike back, because you refuse to do so.

One of the clearest examples of courage in Faulkner's novels occurs in *Go Down, Moses*. Isaac McCaslin is being taught the lore of the wilderness under the tutelage of Sam Fathers, an old man who is part white, part black, and part Indian. Sam has taught Isaac how to find and follow the paw prints of Old Ben, an enormous bear that the hunters, year after year, have failed to bring to bay. On one of their encounters with Old Ben, Isaac has with him a little fyce dog—a yappy mongrel terrier, feisty by name and feisty by nature. The fyce, not much "bigger than a rat" (211), rushes at the bear, and the boy Isaac has to rush after it and pick it up in the very shadow of Old Ben to save it from instant annihilation. But Old Ben exhibits his own sense of chivalry by not attacking either the dog or the boy. He simply slips back into the wilderness. After this incident, Sam addresses the little dog as he strokes it: "You's almost the one we wants. . . . You just aint big enough. We aint got that one yet. He will need to be a little bigger than smart, and a little braver than either" (212). Bravery is bravery, however, and is not to be measured by one's size or strength. Indeed, the little fyce's size proves his bravery to be proportionally all the greater.

On another occasion, one of the young hounds chasing Old Ben dashes in so close to the bear as to have her head raked by the great animal's claws. Later, Sam treats her wounds and muses that the young hound took the risk because she just had to do so in order to prove that she was worthy of being called a hunting dog. Thus, in Faulkner, courage is often, and indeed usually, involved with pride. A man, and, as Sam imagines it, even a dog, fears the danger less than he fears to be thought a coward. One's pride in being a man or a dog is at stake.

I have used animals to illustrate Faulkner's belief in the importance of courage, for Sam Fathers is obviously projecting human qualities onto the animals he loves. But, of course, Faulkner sees moral courage as something far more important than mere animal courage. I shall provide some examples a little later, but I shall postpone them until I have first examined instances of honor and pride.

Honor is a quality that in our day is often misunderstood and even actually frowned upon. The consequence is that many readers simply do not know what Faulkner is talking about when he refers to honor.

That, at least, has been my experience in teaching Faulkner to college students. This is my excuse for defining and clarifying the term. Faulkner, if I understand him, means by honor something very close to self-respect—an unwillingness to stoop to certain actions that a man believes are degrading and contemptible. An honorable man will not lie, for instance, even if his lie could pass undetected or if a lie would gain him an advantage. Moreover, in Faulkner's world, an honorable man will not allow himself to be treated in a fashion that he regards as undermining due respect for himself. Thus, he will not allow himself to be called a liar or accused of some shameful action.

When we demand a certain treatment from others, we, of course, begin to touch upon the more old-fashioned masculine code of honor which insists that one's own self-respect demands that other men accord one a corresponding respect. Thus, a man would not let another accuse him of ungentlemanly conduct, let alone of an actual crime, and if such insults were offered, he would insist on a formal apology or, if that were not forthcoming, on meeting his traducer on the field of honor. With this last situation, we come to the code duello, which lasted longer in the South than it did elsewhere in the nation. But in the earlier decades, we must remember, it was general in the country at large. For example, one of our Founding Fathers, Alexander Hamilton, was killed in a duel in New York, and one of our early presidents, Andrew Jackson, had killed his man in a duel.

A remnant of this older and more violent code makes its appearance in Faulkner's fiction. A little later I will indicate how Faulkner deals with it, but let me first comment on his treatment of the simpler cases: those in which one's own self-respect will not allow him to do certain things, even to an enemy. A telling illustration occurs in Faulkner's magnificent novel, *Light in August*. Byron Bunch is a homely and awkward little man, quite lacking in the social graces, who earns his living working with his hands at the local planing mill. Nevertheless, Byron is a man of honor as well as of compassion. He takes pity on Lena Grove, a young woman who arrives at the mill, heavily pregnant, who tells him that she is looking for her husband, though it soon becomes apparent that the girl is not married to the scamp who has fathered her child. Byron Bunch at once proceeds to protect her and befriend her, and sees her through her accouchement. He even sees to it that the father of the newborn child is brought by a deputy sheriff to the cabin in which Lena is staying. But Brown, the wretched man in question, proves to be utterly irresponsible and completely lacking in a sense of honor. After making a few lame and awkward apologies to Lena, he notices that a window at the back of the room is open; and, realizing that the deputy sheriff will not be able to see him if he climbs out this back window, he suddenly jumps out and bolts.

Byron has been hiding in some bushes toward the back of the house, for he means to see his mission through to the end. When he sees Lena's paramour leap out the window and flee the scene, Byron prepares to intercept him. This is what he says to himself: "'You're bigger than me. . . . But I dont care. You've had every other advantage of me. And I dont care about that neither. You've done throwed away twice inside of nine months what I aint had in thirtyfive years. And now I'm going to get the hell beat out of me and I dont care about that, neither'" (415). Byron, who scorns to take even this contemptible man by surprise, confronts him directly and, true to his own prediction, does have the hell beaten out of him. But after Brown has left him on the ground and has continued in his flight away from his responsibilities to Lena and his child, Byron lies "bleeding and quiet" but with the satisfaction that he has done what every right-minded man would feel that he had to do.

One of Faulkner's most powerful illustrations of bravery—and of very special moral as well as sheer physical bravery—is to be found in the last episode of his novel *The Unvanquished*. This episode also constitutes Faulkner's most brilliant account of what he calls in his Nobel Prize speech the proper subject matter for great literature: the problems of the human heart in conflict with itself. Here the conflict is in the heart of young Bayard Sartoris. Bayard learns that his father has just been shot down by a former business partner, but now a bitter enemy, Ben Redmond. Bayard knows that the whole community expects him to call Redmond to account. At this time the code of reprisal and vengeance was still powerful in the South and nowhere more powerful than in the relatively new country of north Mississippi. The time of the story is the mid-1870s. The region has not really recovered from the effects of the Civil War and the Reconstruction era. Nearly every person close to Bayard certainly expects him to avenge his father: the members of the Colonel's old Civil War troop led by George Wyatt; Bayard's young stepmother; Ringo, the young black man who had been Bayard's childhood companion; and even kindly old Professor Wilkins, under whose tutelage Bayard has been reading law.

But Bayard has his qualms against killing. He takes very seriously the sixth commandment: "Thou shalt do no murder." Although he loved his father, he cannot hide from himself that his father had become a ruthless man, bemused with his dream of creating a little Sartoris empire. Even George Wyatt admits that the Colonel had pushed Redmond too hard. Most of all, Bayard had already once before killed a man. During the closing days of the war, in which there was no law to which one could appeal, Bayard and Ringo, boys of sixteen, had hunted down the bushwhacker who had cold-bloodedly killed Bayard's grandmother. The effect of this experience on the boy has evidently been traumatic, for when Ringo brings Bayard news that the Colonel has been shot down, Bayard has apparently already resolved never to kill again. Yet he respects the community's standards. He does not want to be thought of as a coward.

Jenny Du Pre, Bayard's aunt, begs him not to go into town the next morning, but hers is the only sane and moderate voice that he hears during this evening. She begs her nephew not to insist on living up to the expectations of his father's old cavalry troop or to heed the pleas of his stepmother, Drusilla, whom she calls a "poor hysterical young woman" (276). Aunt Jenny knows that he is no coward. Bayard, however, tells her that he must confront Redmond. "You see," he tells her, "I want to be well thought of" (280). And Aunt Jenny evidently understands that as a man he must do what his honor dictates. So next morning Bayard rides into town and finds George Wyatt and some of the other members of his father's old Civil War cavalry troop already standing by the stairs that lead up to Redmond's law office. Bayard mounts the stairs and enters Redmond's office. He faces there a man freshly shaven and carefully dressed, a man who is "holding a pistol flat on the desk before him, loose beneath his hand" (286). As Bayard walks steadily toward Redmond, Redmond raises the pistol, but Bayard can see that it is pointed away from him. Redmond fires twice. He then walks out of the office, down the stairs, and strides unmolested right through the clump of Wyatt's companions. Evidently he accomplishes it by sheer force of presence and bearing. He goes straight on to the railroad station and leaves town by the train that has just pulled in. He is never seen in Jefferson again.

As for Bayard, he sits down in the office, stunned by the turn of events and emotionally drained until Wyatt and his companions enter. Wyatt says to him: "'My God! . . . You took the pistol away from him and then missed him *twice?*' Then he answered himself—that same rapport for violence which Drusilla had and which in George's case was actual character judgment. 'No; wait. You walked in here without even a pocket knife and let him miss you twice. My God in heaven.' He turned, shouting: 'Get to hell out of here! You, White, ride out to Sartoris and tell his folks it's all over and he's all right. Ride!'" (288).

Even the implacable George Wyatt is won over by Bayard's act, and Drusilla herself comes to acknowledge Bayard's courage, for later, much later, when he enters his bedroom back home, Bayard smells the odor of verbena and finds that Drusilla has left a sprig of verbena on his pillow. It is Drusilla's way of saying, "You were brave," for she always asserted that verbena was the only flower the odor of which could be smelled above the smell of horses. Horses, for Drusilla, were always the steeds of the warrior.

My students often say to me that Bayard repudiated the code of his forebears, and I have to correct them by saying that he does not repudiate but rather transcends the code: that is, he takes all the risks that the code of honor demands, even though he refuses such protection as firing at his opponent might give him.

If Bayard's action exemplifies the way in which bravery and honor were tied together in Faulkner's mind, Bayard's opponent also exemplifies the union of honor and bravery and to the same degree. He has satisfied the claims of honor by giving Bayard full opportunity to execute vengeance on him. If Redmond felt justified in killing Colonel Sartoris, he had evidently resolved not to kill the son. His careful attention to his appearance on the crucial morning makes it plain that he never expected to leave his office alive. Neither, of course, had Bayard. Indeed, we see in the incident the meeting of *two* brave and honorable men.

I have spent a good deal of time in developing the theme of bravery and honor, but of course these were not the only or even the chief values that Faulkner cherished. Pity and love probably stand even higher on his list.

Byron Bunch's compassion for Lena Grove and his concern for her happiness, I have already mentioned. Another Faulkner character of the yeoman white class, V. K. Ratliff, the itinerant sewing-machine agent of Faulkner's *The Hamlet*, is also a man of honor and of compassion. The plight of the idiot Ike Snopes moves him to sympathy and he gives a sum of money to make life somewhat happier for him. A number of Faulkner's women, black as well as white, exemplify pity and maternal concern, and not just for their own children. One of the most signal instances of devoted love and a deeper compassion is to be found in Faulkner's masterpiece, the novel *Absalom, Absalom!*.

Judith Supten is the daughter of a powerful and ruthless man. By his own efforts, her father acquires a hundred square miles of land and builds on it an enormous house, which he means to make a kind of baronial hall. Judith is brought up with all the protective care that one would expect to be given to a girl who is destined to be the chatelaine of a great estate. Soon, however, she meets hardship and even disaster. The handsome young man from New Orleans with whom, after a brief courtship, she had fallen in love, is shot to death just outside the gates of the Sutpen estate, and shot down by Judith's own brother. The two young men had appeared to be the closest of friends and they had served together throughout the four years of the Civil War. Yet now her brother Henry had killed his best friend, Charles Bon, and had done so just before his intended marriage to Judith. Henry does not explain to his sister; he simply flees the country.

A little later, Colonel Sutpen, Judith's father, returns from the war to a ruined plantation. Gone now is any pretense to baronial splendor. Sutpen ekes out a living by setting up a little country general store and Judith is the dutiful daughter who cares for her father until his death. One would not have thought the pair were ever close to each other, but Judith has inherited much of her father's iron will and resolution. She has known that her father had opposed her marriage to Bon, though he has never given her a reason. But her love for Bon has not wavered, and now that Bon is dead, she continues to hold him dear, even after discovering on Bon's dead body a picture of another woman enclosed in the locket that she had supposed contained her own picture.

Later, Judith seeks out Bon's former mistress. She finally locates her in New Orleans and invites her to visit Sutpen's Hundred so that she may see Bon's grave. The woman, a beautiful creature whom Bon had met at the Quadroon Ballroom in New Orleans, does come, and brings with her the child that Bon had fathered. It is a generous act. One might have expected Judith to feel jealousy and a sense of betrayal, for

Bon had paid his court to her without ever hinting that he had ties with another woman who had borne him a son.

A still more generous act is to follow. Judith, later on, sensing somehow that something is amiss, sends her mulatto half-sister, Clytie, to New Orleans to bring back with her Bon's little son, for the mother has indeed recently died. Clytie and Judith undertake to rear the child. On the ruined plantation the two women manage to eke out only a bare living. Judith takes on the heaviest farm work and holds steady the handles of the plow as she plods behind the mule that pulls it.

As he grows up, Bon's son comes to suspect that he is of mixed blood. In his anguish, he repudiates the whole white community and takes as his wife the darkest-hued woman he can find. Judith begs him to go away—to go North, where no one can know his background, where he can make a new life of his own. If he will only do this, Judith promises to look after his wife and son. Although in matters of caste and race Judith is the daughter of her own time and comes quite naturally by its views of the yawning chasm between the black and the white races, she is willing to abrogate the color line.

Judith, however, is unable to persuade the young man to go North and find a new life. Shortly thereafter, he contracts yellow fever. Judith nurses him until his death and then herself succumbs. Judith, as Faulkner conceives her, is a heroic woman—compassionate, loving, possessing a fidelity that triumphs over what would seem to most women a betrayal by her lover. But Judith also powerfully exemplifies another virtue that stands high on Faulkner's list of virtues—the ability to endure all of Fate's buffetings.

In this matter of endurance, we must place beside Judith the black woman Dilsey, of *The Sound and the Fury*. Dilsey is the faithful servant in the Compson household who tries to hold together that crumbling family. It was for Dilsey and her kind that Faulkner penned the resonant epitaph: "They endured" (427). Judith Sutpen and Clytie are also worthy of the same salute to their steadfastness.

Thus far I have talked about the virtues that Faulkner so often stresses in the characters that inhabit his fiction. Yet it occurs to me that something is to be gained by mentioning the negative cases— Faulkner's villains as well as his heroes and heroines. With regard to a writer's spiritual values, one may learn almost as much from what the writer despises as from what he celebrates.

Faulkner has provided us with a God's plenty—or rather, I should say, a devil's plenty—of villains from which to choose. In fact, most of Faulkner's characters have flaws. There are among them no plaster saints. Contrariwise, some of his worst offenders have a few noble traits. Judith Sutpen's father provides a notable example of such a mixture: though he is a hard, ruthless, and self-centered man, he is also courageous and apparently able to endure anything. There are, however, a couple of Faulknerian characters of almost unmitigated depravity: Jason Compson and Flem Snopes. Jason is the wicked presence of *The Sound and the Fury*. One senses that he positively enjoys hurting other people. He is an almost congenital liar; he steals money from his sister; he delights in torturing his young niece who suffers the fate of being brought up in the poisonous atmosphere of the Compson household. Jason's worst trait is this streak of sadism.

Yet, though Jason is perhaps Faulkner's most detestable and sadistic character, I choose to award first place in sheer meanness to Flem Snopes, for Flem, to my mind, represents almost the nadir of human virtue—an abstract zero of the human spirit. Therefore, though Flem seems to be more properly an instance of negativity than of positive malignity, he may best suit my purpose here—which, in brief, is simply to mark the bottom line on Faulkner's scale of human virtues. Thus, Flem comes close to being simply inhuman; yet, just because he is, he can help us see more clearly Faulkner's conception of the human enterprise.

Flem is a sharecropper's son who means to rise from rags to riches. From the very beginning, his only goal is to acquire financial power. Nothing can cause him to deviate. His whole personality streamlines him for efficient movement toward that goal. Flem is a man almost without appetites. He does not drink or smoke, and he is sexually impotent. The ordinary temptations of the senses have no hold on him—neither vices nor innocent pleasures. If Flem ever enjoys a good dinner or a pleasant ride in the country, that fact is never made apparent. Thus, there is nothing to distract him from his pursuit of wealth.

Flem does get married, having been offered a sufficient consideration to marry a wealthy man's daughter who has become pregnant by another man. His marriage is thus simply another matter of business. Since Flem seems to lack all human sympathies, compassion does not deter him from making money wherever the opportunity offers. No widow is too poor, no orphan too helpless, to escape him. Nor are the takings ever too small: every ill-got penny counts. Flem's money-making proclivities are his whole life: that is what the good life means to him—gathering in the dollars or even just the quarters and dimes.

V. K. Ratliff, who knows Flem well and who is a first-rate raconteur in the folk idiom, contrives a very amusing narrative in which he treats Flem as a kind of Faustus, a man who has sold his soul to the Devil in return for his almost magical skill in turning a pretty penny. But as Ratliff sees it, Flem is too shrewd a businessman to have *sold* his soul. He has simply borrowed on it, leaving his soul for security in the Devil's safety-deposit box. Finally, Flem goes down to the infernal regions to pay off the loan and recover his security—that is, his soul. When the soul cannot be immediately produced, one of the junior executives of hell tries to put him off, but Flem stands on his legal rights and demands to have an interview with one of the head devils. This is what ensues—as Ratliff tells it, the junior devils are here speaking to the Prince of Hell:

> "He says a bargain is a bargain. That he swapped in good faith and honor, and now he has come to redeem it, like the law says. And we cant find it," they says. "We done looked everywhere. It wasn't no big one to begin with nohow, and we was specially careful in handling it. We sealed it up in a asbestos matchbox and put the box in a separate compartment to itself. But when we opened the compartment, it was gone. The matchbox was there and the seal wasn't broke. But there wasn't nothing in the matchbox but a little kind of dried-up smear under one edge. And now he has come to redeem it. But how can we redeem him into eternal torment without his soul?"
>
> "Damn it," the Prince hollers. "Give him one of the extra ones. Aint there souls turning up here every day, banging at the door and raising all kinds of hell to get in here, even bringing letters from Congressmen, that we never even heard of? Give him one of them."
>
> "We tried that," they says. "He wont do it. He says he dont want no more and no less than his legal interest according to what the banking and the civil laws states in black and white is hisn. He says he has come prepared to meet his bargain and signature, and he sholy expects you of all folks to meet yourn."
>
> "Tell him he can go then. Tell him he had the wrong address. That there aint nothing on the books here against him. Tell him his note was lost—if there ever was one. Tell him we had a flood, even a freeze." (149–50)

Space precludes my quoting in its entirety the rest of Flem's interview with the Prince of Hell. It will have to suffice to say that Flem's logic and cold-blooded legality overpower Satan himself, and the episode ends with Flem triumphant, seated on the very throne of hell. As Ratliff imagines the final scene, the Prince is leaning forward:

> And now he feels that ere hot floor under his knees and he can feel his-self grab-bing and hauling at his throat to get the words out like he was digging potatoes outen hard ground. "Who are you?" he says, choking and gasping and his eyes a-popping up at him setting there with that straw suitcase on the throne among the bright, crown-shaped flames. "Take Paradise!" the Prince screams. "Take it! take it!" And the wind roars up and the dark roars down and the Prince scrabbling across the floor, clawing and scrabbling at that locked door, screaming. (153)

This story seems to me very funny. But it is serious too. Ratliff (and through him, Faulkner) has found an elaborate way of saying that Flem has no soul, and, in saying so, he indicates that a soulless person like Flem, lacking pity, compassion, concern for others, and all the other ties that link one with the brotherhood of man, is not human at all—a thing as conscienceless as a natural force such as an earthquake or a freezing north wind. In a sense, even vicious Jason Compson, who is worse than Flem, is more nearly human, for he at least feels some things, if they are only jealousy, anger, and hate.

Faulkner's conception of the human being is thus right in the main-stream of the great classical-Judaic-Christian tradition. To become in-capable of love and pity is to read oneself right out of the human race.

Faulkner
and the
Community

Many years ago I attempted to set forth the importance of the community in Faulkner's fiction. I argued that failure to take into account the fact of the Southern sense of community kept many otherwise competent readers from understanding what Faulkner was talking about. For example, if a reader was not aware of the kind of community to be found in Faulkner's Jefferson, he would probably have difficulty in locating the theme of a novel or recognizing the fact of its unity.

I hope that I convinced some of my readers, but the reaction of many ranged from blank incomprehension to testy resistance. I was rapped sharply over the knuckles for defending small-town bigotry and an ingrown and sometimes illiterate provincialism. Clearly, for some of my reviewers, there was little to choose between Sinclair Lewis's Gopher Prairie and Faulkner's Jefferson except that Jefferson's principal feature was not a Main Street but the courthouse square, and that Jefferson relieved its general tedium with an occasional lynching, whereas the dullness of Gopher Prairie was never relieved by anything at all.

Here I have another chance to try again to make a case for the importance of the community in Faulkner's work. But I shall be well advised

Given as a lecture at the 1975 Faulkner Conference at Oxford, Miss., and originally published in slightly different form as "The Sense of Community in Yoknapatawpha Fiction," in *University of Mississippi Studies in English*, XIII (1978).

to try more carefully to define my terms. I could be very scholarly and begin with Professor Ferdinand Tönnies's celebrated distinction between *Gemeinschaft* and *Gesellschaft*. W. H. Auden, however, has put what is essentially the same distinction less abstractly and more engagingly. He starts with the mere crowd. In one of his lectures he describes a cartoon in *The New Yorker*. A huge octopus has just emerged from a manhole in a New York street and is attacking a little guy who is carrying an umbrella. The little guy is using his umbrella to protect himself, and a certain number of people have stopped for a moment to watch the encounter (but nobody is offering help). The caption of the cartoon, as I remember it, was this: "It takes so little to generate a crowd in New York."

Now, this group of onlookers, Auden says, are simply a *crowd*: a random lot of individuals who happen to be near the scene and who stop for a moment to watch. They have nothing in common except nearness to the scene and a brute curiosity. The impersonality of the busy city is nicely caricatured in the fact that nobody offers to help the little man with the umbrella.

The next stage beyond a crowd, Auden points out, is a *society*. Men are drawn together for mutual profit. A town needs so many doctors, so many bakers, so many tailors and candlestick makers; so many advertising men, so many stockbrokers, so many corporation lawyers, not to mention so many con men and so many pickpockets. The ties that bind the members of a society together are finally economic: the relationship of the individuals is functional.

There is nothing, to be sure, wrong with that; but more personal relationships are incidental and ultimately unnecessary. A great American city will frequently contain apartment houses inhabited by people who do not know, and may prefer not to know, the residents in the apartment across the corridor.

The third stage, in Auden's set of categories, is a *community*—a group of people united by common likes and dislikes, aversions and enthusiasms, tastes, way of life, and moral beliefs. The agreement, naturally, is never absolute; but when it is substantial, we have a true community.

Now, it is plain that most communities are also societies. (I am leaving out the specialized communities of a church or a club, or of university professors, or of associations of undertakers, and so on. These are true communities in virtue of their sharing common values, but they are narrowly specialized. It would be a rare city that would consist only of college professors or doctors.) And most communities also have their appropriate complements of firemen, housewives, hardware merchants, garbage men, and so on. But it should also be plain that a functioning society need not be a community, and, indeed, the history of America (and of Europe, for that matter) is of former communities dissolving into mere societies.

The reasons are obvious: the decay of religion, increasing moral relativism, the sheer growth of the cities, industrialization, mechanization—all these factors tend to break up the cohesion generated by common background, traditional beliefs, and close personal associations. The relatively tight small-town and farming communities of the older America have been disappearing. But they had certainly not disappeared from the world in which Faulkner grew up, and they have an important place in the world that he created in his fiction.

I, too, grew up in such a world. I took for granted the values I shared with my fellows. It was only years later that I became fully conscious of the beliefs, values, and attitudes that I shared, quite unreflectingly, with others. For such a sense of community is like the air we breathe. One simply takes it for granted. It is only when one is deprived of that air—when one begins to stifle and gasp—that he realizes its importance. Once we have lost our community—and usually not until we have lost it—do we come to value it, or even see it for what it is.

But what of that large group of Americans today who have never experienced this sort of community? Let me hasten to add that they comprise many of our brightest and best. What do these people do when they confront Faulkner's world? Some of them simply throw up their hands in incomprehension. Some praise Faulkner for what they take to be his campaign to expose social squalor. But some readers do see what is at stake and come to view the communally knit world that is realized in Faulkner's fiction with interest and sympathy. I do not say that their admiration is uncritical. They may be well aware of its limitations and of its occasionally cruel constraints, but they recognize that the loss of cultural cohesion is a genuine loss, all the more so in a world suffering from alienation and atomization.

Was Faulkner himself aware of this cultural cohesion? Do we simply have to take Mr. Brooks's word for it? Does it ever clearly surface in Faulkner's work? Yes, it does. Let me offer a few obvious instances. The nameless narrator of "A Rose for Emily" never says "I thought this" or "I believed that." Throughout the story he uses phrases such as "Our whole town went to her funeral"; "We had long thought"; "We were not pleased exactly, but vindicated"; "We did not say that she was crazy then. We believed she had to do that"; "At first we were glad"; "So the next day we all said." I could continue, but surely it is evident that the man who tells the story of Miss Emily is consciously speaking for the community, and his story is finally about what Miss Emily's life and death meant to the community.

Or look at the opening page of *The Town*. Chick Mallison, who will be one of the several narrators of the novel, is speaking here. And what does he tell the reader as he begins his account? "So when I say 'we' and 'we thought' what I mean is Jefferson and what Jefferson thought." If one wants a much more elaborate—and poignant—account of Chick Mallison's close and sometimes agonizing relation to Jefferson as his own community, he might recall, in *Intruder in the Dust,* the moving description of a boy's pride in his community and his fear that it will not live up to what he has come to demand of it.

Yet, a question calculated to deflate the whole importance of community may come from a diametrically opposite quarter. Let me venture to phrase the form it might take: "All right. Everybody has his familiarity with his own world and maybe a sneaking love for it. If that's all you mean, can't we find it in almost any other modern American writer? Surely, it's no rarity."

Well, let's look at the work of some of Faulkner's contemporaries. We might start with Ernest Hemingway. Typically, the Hemingway novel has to do with an outsider—an American in Spain attending the bull-fights, or an American fighting on the Loyalist side in the Spanish Civil War, or an American on the Italian front in the First World War. The American may even feel the attraction of this foreign society which has its own, and to him, exotic, costumes, rituals, and codes. The Hemingway hero certainly looks on it with interest, and at times even with a certain envy; but he never forgets that it is alien to him, and his very awareness of it enforces his sense of his own isolation.

Yes, some will say, but what about his companions—that group of tough-minded, hard-drinking British and American expatriates that we find, for example, in *The Sun Also Rises*? Don't they themselves constitute a community of which the Hemingway protagonist is a member? They do indeed, but what a special community it is! A brotherhood of the alienated—far away from home in a foreign land, and, more important, men and women who have crossed over some spiritual frontier and have left far behind the value system which was their native heritage. They have looked on the unveiled face of nothingness and have discovered that they must come to terms with it, each by his own strength—without the aid of family, church, and the other traditional supports. They are survivors of a holocaust—the veterans, the initiates.

Or consider F. Scott Fitzgerald. Fitzgerald was a Midwesterner and he allows Nick Carraway, the narrator of *The Great Gatsby,* himself a Midwesterner, to express what are probably Fitzgerald's own personal views when he speaks rather feelingly of "my Middle West," and remarks that he and the other principal characters of the novel found themselves "subtly unadaptable to Eastern life." Nick testifies that the East has for him a certain "quality of distortion." But Fitzgerald, nevertheless, usually writes about the East, about Europe, or about Hollywood—that precinct dedicated to distortion. More important still, he writes about a very special breed of people, the very rich, who, as Fitzgerald once observed to Hemingway, are "not like the rest of us." I am not trying to mark Fitzgerald down because of the material he used, or to give Faulkner extra points because, for the most part, he kept his characters at home. Rather, I am trying to define what I mean when I attribute to Faulkner a sense of community.

Sinclair Lewis did write about his own Middle West, and not always satirically. But Lewis, when he is interested in Main Street at all, is interested in it as a kind of lowest common denominator of American life. It is not so much wicked or vicious as simply negative. The task of the talented individual will be to try to build something on it, but in itself it has almost nothing to contribute. In short, I simply do not find in Gopher Prairie the organic quality evident in Faulkner's Jefferson, and the Gopher Prairieites, mere flat stereotypes, lack the individuality that one finds in I. O. Snopes, or Manfred de Spain, or Henry Armstid, or Jason Compson. I do not know whether this deficiency lay in his hometown, Sauk Centre, Minnesota, or whether Lewis simply failed to recognize what was in fact there. Whatever the explanation, however, there is lacking in Lewis's fictional world anything remotely resembling the sense of community that one discerns in the world of Faulkner. Jefferson is, for better or worse, vibrant with a life of its own; Gopher Prairie is merely a caricature of a town, a parcel of stereotypes, heaped together.

Consider a fourth instance, Sherwood Anderson's *Winesburg, Ohio.* It should prove an instructive one, for its subtitle reads, "A Group of Tales of Ohio Small-Town Life." It was, by the way, a book that Faulkner knew well and admired, calling it Anderson's best work.

Does Anderson's Winesburg represent a community? I think not. Anderson's emphasis is not on a network of relationships that bind the inhabitants together into something like one corporate being. Instead, we are presented with what has to be regarded as a sheaf of case studies—I am not using the term here, by the way, in any derogatory sense—of lonely, frustrated, and alienated people who either are not understood or who at least feel themselves misunderstood by their neighbors and fellow townspeople. Small wonder that, as one critic has put it, most of the Winesburg characters that Anderson writes about seek "release from their frustrations through violence or flight."

Anderson begins his book with a brief introductory section entitled "The Book of the Grotesque," and goes on to tell us that these grotesques, whose stories he is to relate, each had his version of truth— not the whole truth, but what he took to be the truth—and that it was the characters' clinging to their own individual truths that rendered them "grotesques." In short, each of these people had, as Anderson puts it elsewhere, "snatched up one of the truths" which were floating about and had become fixated upon it.

What Anderson is actually telling his reader is that Winesburg was not a community. For, as *community* has been defined earlier, the members of a community share a common truth, make much the same ethical judgments, live by the same codes, and move and have their being in the same basic cultural pattern.

This is my judgment of what Anderson is telling us about Winesburg in his brief introductory section. I am glad to note that Anderson's biographer, James Schevill, makes the same interpretation. I quote his comment upon these grotesques, each of whom exalts his individual truth: "But the truth cannot remain an individual's property," for if it does, "the feeling of the unity, the connection between man and society, is lost." Or, to convert Schevill's terms into those that I am using here, "the sense of community is dissolved."

So much for Winesburg as a true community. Yet I can imagine some readers objecting: "All right, all right. But doesn't Faulkner also write about lonely and alienated people who feel that they are cut off from any community—who believe that the community is unwilling to accept them?" Indeed, Faulkner does write about them. Some of his most interesting and tragic characters belong to this group. But it is a mistake to assume that a writer who has a strong sense of the importance of community is thereby locked into a monotonous affirmation of it or is oblivious to the fact that there are people excluded from it.

Quite the contrary. A concern for community implies a concern for the break with community—whether as a passive isolation from it or active rebellion against it. Since such a writer knows what community is, his notion of what its loss means is also clear. Alienation is not for him some vague malaise, a restlessness and general sense of emptiness. He also probably has a real understanding of the forces that erode the fact of community. Moreover, in presenting to his readers the anguish of his alienated characters, he has one great natural advantage: he can silhouette his alienated characters against the background of a community in being, with all the benefits of contrast and clear definition which such a background affords. In short, he can work, not with abstractions, but with concrete situations.

Of these alleged advantages that Faulkner enjoys, then, let me begin with a fairly simple illustration: the way in which the community of Jefferson dealt with the Reverend Gail Hightower. From the very day of his arrival in Jefferson to become the new minister in the Presbyterian church, Hightower speaks less like a moral and spiritual leader than like a horse trader happy over having made "an advantageous trade." But the elders of the church are patient and long-suffering. They do not make any fuss about his rather odd sermons, full of imagery drawn from the Civil War, about gallantry and glorious deaths in cavalry charges. The congregation soon becomes disturbed, however, by the odd behavior of the minister's wife, and later on, when "in the middle of the sermon, she sprang from the bench and began to scream, . . . shaking her hands toward the pulpit where the husband had ceased talking," they are profoundly shocked. People try to restrain her, but she keeps "shaking her hands" at her husband or at God, until her husband comes down to her. "She stopped fighting then and he led her out, with the heads turning as they passed, until the superintendent told the organist to play. That afternoon the elders held a meeting behind locked doors."

A long-suffering congregation, I should call it, the members of which were concerned and surely sympathetic, but who were bewildered as well. The upshot is that the congregation made up a sum to send the wife to a sanatorium. Hightower continues to preach, and, we are told, some of the women "who had not entered the parsonage in months, were kind to him, taking him dishes [of food] now and then, telling one another and their husbands what a mess the parsonage was in." All very human, but basically kindly. The congregation feels sympathetic toward its pastor and even toward his wife when she returns from the sanatorium to make a new start.

Once again, however, the minister's wife stops coming to church, and finally there is a shocking scandal. She jumps or falls from a window of a Memphis hotel where she and another man had been registered as husband and wife. The city newspapers, of course, are full of it; and yet that very Sunday morning, Hightower enters his church as if nothing had happened and goes "up into the pulpit." When he does so, "the ladies got up first and began to leave. Then the men got up too, and then the church was empty, save for the minister . . . and the Memphis [newspaper] reporters . . . sitting in a line up the rear pew."

A somewhat similar incident occurred in a little Southern town in which I once lived. A prominent merchant had carried on an affair for years with the wife of another prominent citizen. When the affair finally became public, and the merchant had been duly divorced by his wife and his paramour had been divorced by her husband, the guilty pair, one Sunday morning, seated themselves in a church of a different denomination. The organist of the church that was being adopted at once jumped from the organist's bench as if a firecracker had been exploded under her, and rushed out of the church of her fathers, slamming the door as she departed. How many of the rest of the congregation followed her, I do not know. The sinner was wealthy; large contributions could be expected from him; and that may have made it easier to practice the Christian virtue of forgiveness, though, to be sure, the merchant and his new consort did not enter the church as penitents.

Hightower's congregation, however, was presented with something much harder to swallow, let alone digest. What his flock really could not forgive was his intolerable breach of manners. To make matters worse, on the next day Hightower insisted on conducting his wife's burial service, and on the next Sunday, he was in his pulpit again as if nothing had happened. Naturally, he was asked to resign.

If Hightower's congregation had consisted of saints, perhaps they would, through an exercise of Christian *agapē,* have understood and forgiven their minister, ministering to him, discerning his fault—that narcissistic incapacity to love anything except his conception of his role. Or again, if his congregation had all been psychiatrists—but then would any of them have been found attending a Presbyterian church?—they might have set about the long process of effecting a psychoanalytical cure. But Faulkner is dealing here with people possessing no special spiritual vocation, no training in psychiatry, and belonging to an old-fashioned and traditional society. In any case, I am primarily concerned not with Hightower's spiritual pride or his stunted psyche but with the idea of community. The persons in the congregation are not simply a collection of disparate individuals, often at odds with each other. In their attitudes and judgments they tend to act as one body.

What happens later will provide further illustrations. When Hightower is at last persuaded to resign, we are told at this news "the town was sorry with being glad, as people sometimes are sorry for those whom they have at last forced to do as they wanted." They are sorry, and raise a collection to help Hightower get settled elsewhere, but then are again outraged when they find that he has no intention of leaving Jefferson. They let him know that they feel that he acted dishonorably in accepting the money. But then when Hightower offers to return it, the congregation, which has its own sense of honor, scorns taking it back. Many people have now come to harbor bitter feelings against this strange and obstinate man, and scandalous stories about him begin to circulate. Is not Faulkner then, just like Anderson, presenting the case of the alienated individual? Of course he is—and not merely in his depiction of Joe Christmas and of Byron Bunch. But unlike Anderson, Faulkner's focus is on the community, the enveloping social context. In his *Light in August,* for example, Hightower has sinned against the community more than the community has sinned against him. In any case, this essay is concerned with Faulkner's powerful consciousness of the community.

The upshot of the scandalous stories that begin to be whispered about is that several of the more ruffianly characters in the town order Hightower to fire his black woman servant. Hightower refuses to dismiss her, but, conscious of such pressure, she resigns the job, and other black cooks were presumably now afraid to work for the disgraced minister.

Finally, Hightower receives a note, signed "K. K. K.," ordering him to leave town by sunset, and when he does not go, he is abducted, tied to a tree in the woods, "and beaten unconscious." Nearly every close community has its lunatic fringe and individuals who do not stop at violence. But we jump to conclusions if we assume, as some people have, that Faulkner sees the Southern community as constituted of bigoted ruffians. In recounting the story of Hightower, the narrator of the story observes:

> The town knew that [the beating of Hightower] was wrong, and some of the men came to him and tried to persuade him to leave Jefferson, for his own good, telling him that next time [the ruffians] might kill him. But he refused to leave. He would not even talk about the beating, even when they offered to prosecute the men who had done it [if he would divulge their names, but] he would neither tell nor depart. Then [the author tells us] all of a sudden the whole thing seemed to blow away, like an evil wind. It was as though the town realized at last that he would be a part of its life until he died, and that they might as well become reconciled.

The townspeople leave the minister alone and, a little later, since it is evident that he has to do his own cooking and housework, "the neighbors began to send him dishes again, though they were the sort of dishes which they would have sent to a poor mill family. But it was food, and well meant."

I've been so detailed with this episode because it illustrates so much. In the first place, it dramatizes the general solidity of the community: there are some issues that do not have to be debated; many community reactions seem almost instinctive. On the other hand, the community is not one undifferentiated bloc; there are gradations in emphasis and accordingly in judgments about what to do; there are those whose feelings and reactions become violent, though most of the members of the community repudiate any brutal enforcement of the community's will. Finally, one observes that the community is not locked into one doctrinaire attitude. The prevailing attitude toward Gail Hightower shifts from incomprehension to pity to outrage to slanderous bitterness to a revulsion from such bitterness to pity again, and finally to a kind of tolerant acceptance. In short, the members of the community are not ideologues who follow a party line or the behests of an executive committee. Instead, the community's changing views resemble the changing attitudes of an individual who, though he can be driven to outrage and anger, is fundamentally decent and compassionate.

Let's turn to another novel, *Absalom, Absalom!*. The Jefferson community in the 1830s or 1840s was rather different from the Jefferson community seen a century later in *Light in August*. The earlier Jefferson was much closer to frontier days. The Indians had only recently departed and the blacks were still enslaved. Yet it is a true community and it does not radically differ from what it will become a century later.

How does it treat the mysterious outsider, Thomas Sutpen, who comes into Jefferson from God knows where, and who, because of his strange conduct, arouses the worst suspicions? The town, for example, speculates about Sutpen's wagonload of black slaves who speak some strange tongue that is not English, about his foreign-born architect, about his vast landholdings, and about how he obtained them.

They cannot make him out—why does he want to build a great mansion; why, having completed it, does he leave it unfurnished for some years; and perhaps most of all, why does he not look for a wife among the neighboring planter families but instead courts the elder daughter of a rather straitlaced storekeeper in the town?

When, after a three months' absence, he returns with four wagons loaded with household furnishings, one citizen of the little town exclaims: "Boy, this time he stole the whole durn steamboat!" The opinion is taken seriously; a posse gathers, and Sutpen is arrested. Note that he is arrested and arraigned. It is not a matter of a mob gathering and calling for a rope. But two of the town's most respectable citizens stand up for him—Mr. Coldfield, whose daughter Sutpen is courting, and General Compson, a prominent planter. They sign Sutpen's bond, and not long after, Sutpen is married to Ellen Coldfield.

The community, however, is still very suspicious of Sutpen. No more than a half dozen people, aside from General and Mrs. Compson and Mr. Coldfield and his sister-in-law, come into the little Methodist church to witness the wedding ceremony—and when the bride and groom emerge, the crowd that has gathered throw clods and vegetable refuse at Sutpen. We are told that this group consist of "the traders and drovers and teamsters." Yet, even they apparently intend no serious injury, and even from among this riff-raff a voice is heard to shout, "Look out! Don't hit her now!" These ruffians, moreover, are transients. The stable folk of the community do not throw anything or even jeer. They sit silently in their carriages, though curiosity has brought them out as if "to see a Roman holiday."

Later, however, these people relax sufficiently to drive out to Sutpen's Hundred to pay calls, and the men to hunt his game. They also come out, from time to time, to watch Sutpen, having stripped to the waist, fight with his slaves.

They observe with wonder: his ways are clearly not their ways, but they are not blind to his virtues—his energy, his courage, his determination. His neighbors finally accept him, we are told, grudgingly, perhaps, with reservations, as a kind of licensed eccentric. Nevertheless, it is acceptance. In times of stress, they actually elect him colonel of the local regiment, ousting Colonel Sartoris to do so. But the author of the novel also makes it clear that Sutpen preserves his fierce independence and makes no concessions to the community: there is a specific reference to Sutpen's "utter disregard of how his actions" must appear to the town. We are told further that in the town Sutpen never had but one friend, General Compson. Even his father-in-law came to fear and distrust him.

How important is it for the reader to take note of Sutpen's real relation to the community? Very important, I should say. A real comprehension of this relationship would have prevented the printing of a good deal of nonsense—about the true springs of Sutpen's actions, about whether he is the heroic individual defying an essentially morbid society, or whether he is the very embodiment of that morbid society. The truth is that his relation to the community into which he has come is in fact very mixed and ambiguous. Accurate information on that point clarifies some of the basic themes of the novel.

But let me move to a simpler case. I've already noted that the narrator of "A Rose for Emily" is, though nameless, clearly a spokesman for the community, and surely his telling the story from the community's viewpoint implies that it had a meaning for that community. It is true that the narrator never spells out the meaning, but a sensitive reader of the story ought to be able to infer it. Miss Emily does possess the aristocratic virtues. Her proud independence and disregard for bureaucratic regulation elicit a certain admiration from the community itself— particularly as that community finds itself more and more pushed toward timid uniformity. But Miss Emily's absolute defiance of what others think, and her insistence on meeting life solely on her own terms, ignoring custom, tradition, and law, can end in a horrifying deformation of her own psyche. The community learns *how* horrifying only after Miss Emily's death when the door of an upstairs bedroom is forced and the intruders discover what is left of the body of her lover of forty years before.

A refusal to knuckle under to the forms and actions expected by the community need not, of course, be disastrous. But complete isolation from the community can lead to madness and murder. If, however, we subtract all such elements from Miss Emily's story, we pretty well reduce it to a clinical report in abnormal psychology—which is where a good many critics have left it. Yet, clearly, the feelings of the community toward Miss Emily are richly complicated. For the community, her story is no mere case history. It comes close to being a legend, a fable, even a parable.

Isolation from the community and its consequences figure powerfully in the story of Joe Christmas in *Light in August*. If, as so many insist on doing, we make the primary theme of the novel race prejudice, we shall miss a great deal of the novel's richness and its bearing upon larger issues. We shall also oversimplify the plight of Joe Christmas himself. For Joe lives not merely in a state of defiance of the white community. He repudiates the black community too. He has no difficulty in passing for a white man, and there is no hard evidence in the novel that he possesses any Negro genes whatsoever. But Joe finds himself at home in neither the white world nor the black. Joe has in fact tried to live both as a white man and as a black. Neither works for him. Instead, he finds himself a man suspended between the two, bereft of any community. Joe's sense of unrest and homelessness, the reasons for which Faulkner articulates so carefully, is not a matter of his genes at all, but of a warped psyche. In this general matter he resembles Gail Hightower and Emily Grierson, and Faulkner has told Joe's story, like theirs, against the background of a vital community—

not, let me repeat, a model community, not a community of saints or of happily adjusted liberal sociologists, but a group of people who share customs, beliefs, and social rituals—a community, in short, that provides a contrasting backdrop for the sometimes heroic but always lonely and often disastrous life of each of these spiritually lost souls.

The community in Faulkner, however, is more than a mere backdrop to the individual's lonely struggle, and the pressure it exerts upon the individual does not necessarily end in disaster. One example of what I mean has to do with the coming to maturity of young Bayard Sartoris as told in *The Unvanquished*. The culminating incident was outlined earlier.

In teaching this story, I have frequently had to clear up a serious misapprehension. Students who have a contempt for what they take to be a barbarous and backward community have difficulty seeing Bayard's problem. How could it ever have occurred to him to think of killing Redmond? A sensible man would simply have turned matters over to the district attorney and perhaps hired some extra counsel to back up the prosecution, but certainly not risked his own life in a foolhardy gesture of outmoded gallantry. Of course, it would never occur to these same students to apply such reasoning to Shakespeare's *Hamlet*. The application of such modern standards and attitudes would destroy an appreciation not only of *Hamlet* but of *The Iliad, Oedipus Rex, The Song of Roland,* not to mention other classics. Yes, someone says, but *The Unvanquished* is different: it's about modern America.

But, of course, it is not about modern America. North Mississippi a century ago was a very different world from that of modern America. An important difference is its strong sense of community and of a community of a special kind, characterized by powerful family and clan loyalties, by an almost quixotic code of personal honor, and by a cult of physical and moral bravery.

In short, if we are to grasp the full quality of Bayard's moral heroism, we have to understand the power of the force that he had to resist. Indeed, we cannot do justice to any of the characters—Drusilla, Colonel Sartoris, George Wyatt, or even Redmond—unless we know what the issues were for them.

One final item about the Yoknapatawpha community. I have pointed out that it is not monolithic, and I would now point out further that it is not petrified into rigidity. When George Wyatt, the somewhat illiterate man of yeoman stock, grasps what Bayard has done, he says, "You ain't done anything to be ashamed of. I wouldn't have done it that way, myself. I'd a shot at him once, anyway. But that's your way or you wouldn't have done it."

So even Wyatt accepts Bayard's transcendence of the older code; and so does even Drusilla, whom Faulkner has described as "the priestess of a succinct and formal violence." She has gone away, presumably never to return. But she left the verbena on his pillow, in acknowledgment and acceptance of the heroism of his action.

Faulkner's
Early Attempts
at the Short Story

One has to be very charitable not to dismiss as mere hackwork the character sketches and short short-stories that Faulkner published in the *Double Dealer* and the New Orleans *Times-Picayune* in 1925. Furthermore, one can scarcely plead in extenuation of their awkwardness the youthfulness of the author, for Faulkner was writing his very promising first novel, *Soldiers' Pay,* during the very months that saw the publication of these New Orleans sketches.[1] *Soldiers' Pay* was not in the least inept. It is in fact a quite remarkable piece of work and was regarded as such by most of those who reviewed it in 1926. By contrast, nearly all the short stories that the young writer contributed to the *Times-Picayune* are trivial, and the writing is forced and artificial where it is not simply hackneyed.

The principal interest in these sketches lies, as a matter of fact, in their foreshadowings of what was to come in the later works. Carvel Collins has dealt with the more important of these anticipations in his

Originally published in slightly different form as "A Note on Faulkner's Early Attempts at the Short Story," in *Studies in Short Fiction,* X (1973).
    1. Carvel Collins chose *New Orleans Sketches* as the title for his collection of all this New Orleans material, which Random House published in 1958. Although the *Double Dealer* vignettes resemble Theophrastian "characters," the *Picayune* series are best described as short short-stories. However abbreviated and jejeune, they attempt to do more than merely depict a type; they embody a definite narrative line. Compare "The Cobbler" (four paragraphs) published in the *Double Dealer* with "The Cobbler" (twelve paragraphs) as published in the *Times-Picayune.*

excellent introduction to *Sketches*. What I shall be concerned with in this essay will be some of the literary influences that they manifest.

One might expect to see in them the impress of Sherwood Anderson, since Faulkner and Anderson were both living in New Orleans during the early months of 1925 and Anderson had encouraged the younger man to pursue a literary career and was directly responsible for the publication of his first novel. But no obvious reflection of Anderson's style occurs in the New Orleans sketches—or in *Soldiers' Pay*, for that matter—and there is sufficient reason why there should not be.

Although Faulkner liked Anderson as a person and admired intensely aspects of his work, he judged Anderson to be lacking in literary sophistication. During the very period in which Faulkner was seeing him almost daily in New Orleans, he declared in print that Anderson—who by this time had published some nine books and was in his fiftieth year—had "not matured yet."[2] Even *Winesburg, Ohio*, for which Faulkner had high praise, "would have become mawkish," so Faulkner observed, "had [it] been done as a full-length novel." But "the gods had looked out for him": they had told him where to stop. In the very next year, 1926, Faulkner published a parody of Anderson's style. The parody is rather innocently amusing and not cruel, as was Hemingway's takeoff on Anderson in *The Torrents of Spring*, but the fact of the parody makes quite clear that the young Faulkner had fully emancipated himself from any disposition to imitate Anderson.[3] In 1927 appeared *Mosquitoes*, where under the name of Dawson Fairchild, Anderson comes in for detailed analysis of his naïveté and literary shortcomings—though it must be conceded that some of Anderson's real virtues are also given their due.

Although one would not, in view of Faulkner's keen sense of Anderson's special limitations as a literary artist, expect to find obvious instances of his influence in Faulkner's writings, yet in one special way Anderson's example, I believe, did help shape the New Orleans sketches

2. See his essay on Anderson published by the Dallas *Morning News*, April 26, 1925. Carvel Collins reprints it in *William Faulkner: New Orleans Sketches*.

3. See *Sherwood Anderson & Other Famous Creoles* (New Orleans, 1926). Anderson's feelings were hurt, and the two men were out of touch with each other henceforward, but Anderson continued to express a high opinion of Faulkner's talents (see Michael Millgate, *The Achievement of William Faulkner* [London, 1965], 17–20) and Faulkner, in 1953, published a handsome tribute to Anderson (see James B. Meriwether, *Essays, Speeches, and Public Letters by William Faulkner* [New York, 1965], 3–10).

and some of Faulkner's stories published elsewhere during the early 1930s.

In the first section of *Winesburg, Ohio,* entitled "The Book of the Grotesque," the storyteller says: "It was the truths that made the people grotesques. The old man had quite an elaborate theory concerning the matter. It was his notion that the moment one of the people took one of the truths to himself, called it his truth, and tried to live his life by it, he became grotesque and the truth he embraced became a falsehood." Most of the inhabitants of Winesburg are grotesques in this sense; many, though by no means all of them, are frustrated, unhappy, and defeated people. Yet as the storyteller observes, the "grotesques were not all horrible. Some were amusing, some almost beautiful, and one, a woman all drawn out of shape, hurt the old man by her grotesqueness."

The stories implied by the sketches that Faulkner published in the *Double Dealer* tell of loss or hurt or aspirations still to be fulfilled. The more fully developed narratives that appeared in the *Times-Picayune* have as their principal characters people who can fairly be called "grotesques" even in Anderson's sense:[4] the little racehorse tout of "Mirrors of Chartres Street"; Jean-Baptiste, who, angry and disappointed with his life in America, means to rob a bank and who is deterred from crime because he hears someone on the street playing a familiar Provençal air; the insanely suspicious husband of "Jealousy"; or the little jockey of "Cheest!."

Like Anderson's grotesques, Faulkner's New Orleans characters have had their sorrows and frustrations. There is the priest who has not been able to sublimate his sexual longings; there is the cobbler who cannot forget the beautiful land of Tuscany in which he had been born; there is the old couple in "Episode" who live by begging. Even so, all these people have their imaginations and memories, which, if painful, are also still available, rich, and meaningful. The old couple, for example, relive their earlier life so well in memory that they can still

---

4. W. L. Phillips has pointed out that Anderson's *Winesburg, Ohio* is "peopled by characters whose twisted lives interlock to form a tangled myth of the grotesque" and has argued that the "method of Faulkner's Yoknapatawpha is an elaboration of the *Winesburg* method" (see his "Sherwood Anderson's 'Two Prize Pupils,'" *University of Chicago Magazine,* XLVII [January, 1955], 12). Of the latter statement I am not so sure: Yoknapatawpha has some strange characters, but few are grotesques in Anderson's sense and even they are much more than grotesques. My argument here is that the characters of the New Orleans sketches and of some of the early stories are grotesques on Anderson's model.

retain a glow that attracts the attention of the artist who sees them still alive with fulfilled meaning. They are not grayed over with the pathos that settles over so many of the inhabitants of Anderson's small town in the Middle West.

A comparison of the pieces collected in *New Orleans Sketches* with the stories published by Faulkner in 1930–1931 reveals a remarkable advance. Even if we regard *Sketches* as a perfunctory effort and not representative of Faulkner's full powers at the time, the growth in his artistic power between 1925 and 1930 is spectacular. From the fumblings of "Jealousy" or "Damon and Pythias Unlimited" he had arrived at the brilliant accomplishment of "Dry September" and "A Rose for Emily."

Some of these early stories,[5] notably "Miss Zilphia Gant," "Smoke," "Dry September," and "A Rose for Emily," can tell us a great deal about the young author who had not yet found but was soon—just in the early 1930s—beginning to find a market for his short stories. In the first place, they show him settling into his native territory, and some of the credit for this nudge in the proper direction ought to go to Anderson. Faulkner recalled that Anderson had told him—presumably in 1925 during their association in New Orleans: "You're a country boy; all you know is that little patch up there in Mississippi where you started from" but assured him that this was sufficient for a proper subject matter.[6]

In this connection it may be significant that the most powerful of the New Orleans sketches, "The Liar," has nothing to do with New Orleans at all, but has its setting in the backcountry; moreover, its principal characters, Ek and Lafe, possess good Yoknapatawpha names. The full-scale early stories "Miss Zilphia Gant" and "A Rose for Emily" are also associated with Jefferson and Yoknapatawpha County.

"Smoke" too has a Yoknapatawpha setting, but though it is the weakest of these early Yoknapatawpha stories, it has a certain importance as indicating the influence on Faulkner of a popular short-story

5. It is impossible—at least at the present time—to date precisely the composition of Faulkner's stories. But there is extant a record of Faulkner's attempt to place his stories with magazines in which James B. Meriwether has ascertained that the earliest dated attempt (to place "Idyll in the Desert") was "before Jan. 23, 1930" and the latest of the stories to be discussed in this essay ("A Rose for Emily") was "before March 25, 1930" (see his *Literary Career of William Faulkner* [Princeton, 1961], 173, 174). I am assuming that these stories were probably written during 1929, though of course the date might have been earlier.

6. Meriwether, *Essays, Speeches,* 8.

writer of the time, an influence that has hitherto gone unnoticed, that of Irvin S. Cobb (1876–1944). Cobb was almost as gimmicky as O. Henry—whose general influence suffuses the New Orleans sketches—and quite as lightweight in his presentation of character and theme. But he was immensely popular: Faulkner as a young man must have read his *Cosmopolitan* and *Saturday Evening Post* stories, and Cobb's example may have helped confirm Faulkner in using what was to become his characteristic material. Although Cobb was born in Paducah, Kentucky, the culture reflected in his stories, that of western Kentucky, is continuous with that of west Tennessee and north Mississippi. The special heroes of many of Cobb's stories are Confederate veterans, most of whom had served with General Nathan Bedford Forrest. Forrest is, of course, the special Confederate hero of north Mississippi and of a number of Faulkner's own Civil War stories.

The character who dominates a number of Cobb's early stories is old Judge Priest. The judge, a Civil War veteran, like Faulkner's Judge Dukinfield in "Smoke," has a faithful Negro servant on whom he depends utterly and who is his veritable shadow. Faulkner's Judge Dukinfield and his servant Joe owe, I suspect, a good deal to Cobb's Judge Priest and his servant Jeff Poindexter.

One of the mysteries of Judge Dukinfield's death is how the murderer could have got unobserved past Uncle Joe dozing in his "wire-mended splint chair" in the passageway to the Judge's office. Judge Priest's Jeff also is known to doze while he waits for the old judge to gather up his papers toward quitting time. He can doze even while leaning "against a bookrack" in the Judge's office.

Judge Priest has also probably left his impress on the man who manages to solve Dukinfield's murder: Gavin Stevens. Gavin is a much younger man than Priest and he boasts degrees from Harvard and Heidelberg. But though lacking in impressive degrees, Judge Priest is something of a scholar. At all events he is a sound student of human nature, a wise counselor, and as such he is accorded great respect by the community in which he lives. Like Gavin Stevens, Judge Priest is also an amateur detective, and one of Cobb's books about Priest is actually entitled *Judge Priest Turns Detective*.

There are some fairly specific parallels that may indicate Faulkner's—perhaps unconscious—borrowings from Cobb. One of Cobb's stories tells how a Confederate veteran, on his way home from Virginia, was killed by bushwhackers in the mountains of east Tennessee, just as in Faulkner's "Mountain Victory," Major Saucier Weddel, returning from the Virginia campaigns to his home in Mississippi, is killed by a Unionist mountaineer as he makes his way through east Tennessee. Judge Priest has a cook who, like that admirable woman who looks after the Compson family in *The Sound and the Fury,* is named Dilsey. In *Soldiers' Pay,* Faulkner tells us that Cadet Love's eyes were "like two oysters." I had always supposed that he was remembering Joyce's description of John Henry Menton's "oyster eyes" and perhaps he was. But a character in Cobb's "The Life of an Ant" has an eye "the color of a boiled oyster," and Cobb could not have borrowed from Joyce. His story antedates *Ulysses* by seven years.

Parallels of the sort I have mentioned are in themselves trivial, and are cited here merely to point out the connection. But one device that Faulkner possibly borrowed from Cobb has real importance. Almost all of Cobb's Judge Priest stories are told in the first person by a well-informed member of the community. The teller himself is not involved in the plot and his fortunes are not at stake, but he is a good observer and something of a raconteur. Such a mode of narration is the staple device in the stories printed not only in *Knight's Gambit,* where it is Gavin Stevens who plays detective, but in many other Faulkner stories, including such early ones as "Miss Zilphia Gant" and "A Rose for Emily." Whereas Cobb uses the device perfunctorily and sometimes almost absentmindedly, Faulkner employed it intelligently and responsibly. In Faulkner's skillful hands, such a narrator of the story—often a mere nameless observer—takes on something of the quality of the Sophoclean chorus, voicing the expectations and anxieties of the community and reflecting—often to the great benefit of the reader's comprehension—the community's values and basic assumptions.

"Idyll in the Desert," though it does not have a Yoknapatawpha setting, is told by a minor character. "Idyll" is a story of romantic love in which an older women deserts her home and its comforts to go out to Arizona to nurse her lover, a younger man thought to be dying of tuberculosis. After he recovers and goes back to the East, she stays on at the desolate camp for ten years, in the firm faith that he will someday return to her. (Such is the faith of Alice Hindman in *Winesburg, Ohio.*) Meantime, she has contracted the disease herself; and at the end of the story, her lover, on a wedding trip with his new bride, passes without noticing a figure lying on a stretcher beside the railroad track in an Arizona town. It is the woman who had nursed him back to health, now waiting to be put on a train that will take her to a Los Angeles hospital and her death. We do not learn enough about the older woman or about her lover to credit completely the sacrifice that she makes or to find any basis for her confidence that he will return to her. In any case, the meeting at the end involves a most improbable coincidence.

Yet it is interesting to observe Faulkner's method for persuading the reader to believe in the situation and in his characters. Here the narrator, Crump, the Arizona mail rider, is something of a wit and a teller of yarns full of humorous exaggeration. He is obviously highly sympathetic with the woman who has sacrificed herself, and yet the detachment that he maintains does a good deal to avoid the sort of sentimentality that would be ruinous. This method of narration (by an outsider who is a remarkable teller of yarns) was to become a favorite method for Faulkner. His great narrator is, of course, V. K. Ratliff.

In "Miss Zilphia Gant," Faulkner also makes use of this device, and here its effectiveness is enhanced by the fact that the narrator is a member of the community. He is not close to Miss Gant, but he is interested in her strange life, and reflects, admirably though quietly, the impact on the community of her scandalous and outrageous story.

Mrs. Gant, Zilphia's mother, is a grotesque in Sherwood Anderson's sense. Her powerful, neurotic personality forces her daughter into a like grotesque distortion. The "truth" that Mrs. Gant grasps and proceeds to build her life around is that men are not trustworthy. When her own husband runs off with another woman, Mrs. Gant leaves her daughter with a neighbor, goes out with a borrowed pistol, executes summary vengeance on the guilty couple, and then returns to her dressmaking shop and devotes her energies to protecting her daughter from men. Faulkner's story might have been entitled "The Daughter of the Amazon," for this fierce and narrow woman, though she wanted a daughter and is passionately devoted to her, hates all males. She succeeds in warping her daughter away from the marriage that might have saved her for a normal life. Faulkner was very much interested in the theme of repression and the effect of an unnatural environment upon a growing child. He was to make powerful use of this kind of conditioning in his account of Joe Christmas in *Light in August*. The psychic wounds that Joe received first from his being brought up in an orphanage and, later, from his foster parents set him at war with the world forever after.

Faulkner is also in this story much concerned with the psychology of terror, especially with the state of a person who is trapped and awaiting the blow. Miss Zilphia tells herself: "Something is about to happen to me" and, in doing so, anticipates Temple Drake's unbelieving comment on her own state of mind: "Something is happening to me."

"Miss Zilphia Gant," however, looks forward more immediately to another early but much abler story, "A Rose for Emily," a horror story regarded as one of the most "gothic" that Faulkner ever wrote. But the reader misses the meaning of the story if all that he derives from it is an experience of horror for its own sake. As in "Miss Zilphia Gant," the narrator is a citizen of the town, but he speaks in a much fuller way for the community than does the man who tells Miss Zilphia's story.

Miss Emily, like Miss Zilphia, has been warped by family repression less spectacularly than Miss Zilphia and in a more plausible way. For Miss Emily is not the child of a mad Amazon who kills her husband and protects her daughter with a shotgun. She is the daughter of a selfish, dominating father, proud of his family name, who thinks that none of the young men who call on his daughter is good enough for her and who succeeds in driving them all away. When he dies—his wife has long been dead—Miss Emily stays on in the old shabby-genteel house and goes mad, gradually and almost imperceptibly.

In one of the *Winesburg, Ohio* stories, Alice Hindman, twenty-seven years old and unmarried, who did "not want Ned Currie or any other man" but who did want "to be loved," undresses on a rainy night, goes out of her empty house onto the streets of the little town, and walks and then runs naked in the rain. Later, inside her room, she asks herself: "What is the matter with me? I will do something dreadful if I am not careful." Turning her face "to the wall, [she] began trying to force herself to face bravely the fact that many people must live and die alone, even in Winesburg."

Anderson's story "Adventure" is as typical of his work as Faulkner's story of Miss Emily Grierson is of his, and both Alice and Emily are sisters of the woman in *The Waste Land* who cries out: "What shall I do now? What shall I do?/I shall rush out as I am, and walk the street/ With my hair down, so. What shall we do to-morrow?/What shall we ever do?"

Repression and neurosis, boredom and despair: these are some of the recurrent themes of twentieth-century literature. But every genuine artist will express them in his own way: Eliot's rich woman is bored and hysterical; Anderson's Winesburg spinster, mildly neurotic; Faulkner's Miss Emily, quietly mad. But madness in the hands of a true artist can be rendered meaningful. Faulkner's special device for rendering it so in "A Rose for Emily" is his use of the unnamed narrator, in this instance, a perceptive and intelligent observer of Miss Emily's bizarre life who is at the same time an eloquent—though in a quiet and understated way—mouthpiece for the community which is scarcely aware of the deep ambiguity of its attitude toward her. The narrator can provide us with an insight into that attitude and can make the perceptive reader understand why the Jefferson community accords Miss Emily, at the end, something of the dignity of a tragic character who may transgress greatly and terribly as, for example, Oedipus did, yet who nevertheless commands a certain awed admiration.[7]

7. R. P. Warren and I have discussed these issues in *Understanding Fiction* (New York, 1950).

Faulkner's
Two Cities

Faulkner's connections with Memphis and with west Tennessee were early and intimate. For Faulkner's hometown, Oxford, Mississippi, Memphis was the great market town, the largest nearby emporium where you shopped for all manner of things, from men's suits and neckties to plows and cotton-gin machinery; and of course it was also the market through which you ultimately sold your cotton or other staple crops.

Everyone knows the saying that Mississippi has two great cities, Memphis and New Orleans, both outside the state. At long last the cities of Mississippi are growing, but are still nowhere near as large as the Tennessee and Louisiana metropolises.

Faulkner in time came to know New Orleans well. On him, as on most young people from the Anglo-Saxon South, New Orleans exerted the charm of the exotic. Its culture is still Latin and Roman Catholic; to the Protestant Southerner it seems delightfully, even wickedly, relaxed and easygoing. Its architecture is attractively Old World and so is its Creole cuisine.

Faulkner spent some exciting and wonderfully creative months in New Orleans, and three of his novels reflect a New Orleans setting. Yet if one examines the index of Joseph Blotner's massive biography of

Given as a lecture in 1981 in Memphis.

Faulkner, the references to Memphis outnumber those to New Orleans, two to one. There are well over a hundred references to Memphis.

For William Faulkner, Memphis was the place you went to for various reasons. He was fond of his great-aunt, Mrs. Walter B. McLean, who lived in Memphis, and he had a good friend there, Arthur Halle, the son of Phil Halle, at whose men's clothing store I remember my mother sometimes shopped for me when my family lived in Collierville.

Faulkner also visited Memphis to enjoy the night life and even the Memphis underworld. His knowledge of it, as reflected particularly in the accounts in *Sanctuary* of Miss Reba's establishment, was substantial—and circumstantial. He seems, to borrow a telling phrase from Matthew Arnold, to be writing about it with his eye on the object. How much of that knowledge was acquired from friends and acquaintances and how much from personal experience, I shall not undertake to say, for the very good reason that I do not know.

Yet, vivid as are his descriptions of these tarnished people and their tawdry surroundings, Faulkner does not make Temple Drake's life in Miss Reba's brothel seem glamorous and attractive. One could fairly claim that Faulkner's *Sanctuary* is finally a moral book. I think it is, but that is not to say that it is platitudinous. There is even some comedy in it, as when the three madams get drunk on beer and sentimentalize about us poor girls who get all the blame and who remark on how sweet the slain gangster looked lying in his expensive coffin.

Because of the furor raised about *Sanctuary,* I suspect that a good many Memphians in the early 1930s felt that the fair name of the city had been besmirched by this young upstart from Mississippi. Actually, a great many of Faulkner's fellow citizens in Oxford smarted under the same sense of disparagement. They took Faulkner to be a sociologist rather than a writer of fiction. This mistake is unfortunate, though many people today continue to confuse fiction with forms of discourse that have very different purposes.

Yet Faulkner's intention was not to blacken the reputation of either Oxford or Memphis, or of his native South, and people have largely come to understand this. Oxford is now very proud of its native son, and I expect that Memphis shares in this pride. In any case, Memphis obviously meant much more to Faulkner than its brothel keepers, bootleggers, and criminals. A hasty review of his fiction will clearly indicate how thoroughly the city of Memphis is interwoven in all of his novels and short stories.

Thus, in *Sartoris*, Miss Jenny Du Pre, the redoubtable aunt of Bayard Sartoris, subscribes to the Memphis afternoon paper, which must have been the *Press-Scimitar*. We are told her reason for choosing it: the author writes that Miss Jenny "enjoyed humanity in its more colorful mutations, preferring lively romances to the most impeccable of dun fact; so she took in the more lurid afternoon paper, even though it was yesterday's when it reached her." No sobersides *Commercial Appeal* for her. Later, when her nephew Bayard gets a peculiar wen on his face, naturally it is to a Memphis specialist that she takes him to be treated.

Sartoris deals with the situation of north Mississippi vis-à-vis Memphis in the early 1920s. But something like this situation had been true as early as the 1850s. In the novel *Absalom, Absalom!* when Thomas Sutpen's daughter Judith is to marry a handsome young man from New Orleans, it is to Memphis that her mother takes her to buy her trousseau. We learn from the novel *The Town*—the time would be the 1920s—that Professor W. C. Handy, composer of "St. Louis Blues" and "The Beale Street Blues," would come down from Memphis to provide the music for a dance.

Out of Memphis, newspaper reporters could descend on Jefferson, Mississippi, when it was discovered that the Reverend Gail Hightower's wife had either jumped or been pushed from a window of a Memphis hotel room that she had occupied with a man other than her husband. Memphis reporters filled the rear pew in Hightower's church that Sunday morning as the congregation walked out in indignation when they discovered that their preacher was going to ascend the pulpit as if nothing extraordinary had happened the night before.

In the Compson Appendix, which Faulkner supplied for a later printing of *The Sound and the Fury*, the faithful black woman Dilsey, who had tried to prop up the collapsing white family, has finally retired to Memphis to live out her days in the household of her daughter Frony. The movement of the blacks off the farms and into the cities was already gaining momentum.

In *Go Down, Moses* it is to Memphis that the men out on a bear hunt send the feckless half-Indian Boon Hogganbeck to get more supplies, mostly liquid in nature. Fortunately, they send with Boon the youthful

Isaac McCaslin, really to keep tabs on Boon. The pair have already missed one train back to Mississippi before Isaac can get his brawny companion on a train headed home. Boon is carrying a good deal of whiskey inside him as well as outside.

Yet these examples are of the nature of references and allusions. Did Faulkner not ever use Memphis as the setting for a novel—that is, aside from his use of it in *Sanctuary*? Yes, he did. That very interesting last novel entitled *The Reivers* makes considerable use of a Memphis setting. So do three of Faulkner's earliest stories. In my opinion, they are not the worst stories that he ever wrote, though they remained unpublished until 1979, when all of his hitherto uncollected stories finally appeared in one volume.

The first of them is called "The Big Shot." In it we have preliminary sketches of two characters later to be prominent in *Sanctuary,* Red and Popeye (who takes his name from an actual person of the Memphis underworld, Popeye Pumphrey). The plot has to do with Mr. Martin, a sharecropper's son, who has moved to Memphis and become wealthy as a contractor and as a manipulator of politicians. The story describes Martin's efforts to bribe Dr. Blount to include his daughter's name in the list of those invited to the Chickasaw Guards Ball, where the debutantes of the year are presented.

Then Faulkner revised this story radically, though preserving the main plot. This time he chose the title "Dull Tale." I think that he much improved the story in the revision, though it still did not sell. The two main characters remain the same as before, Martin and Blount, but the annual coming-out ball has now become the Nonconnah Guards Ball. "Nonconnah" and "Chickasaw" are, I assume, familiar names to all Memphians. Nonconnah Creek is to the south of the city.

The third unpublished story with a Memphis setting is "A Return." In this story, though the plot has been completely changed, Dr. Blount reappears once more as a principal character and again as the person who presides over the coveted invitation list for the Nonconnah Guards Ball.

My list of Faulkner's references to Memphis makes no pretension to completeness. But it need not be exhaustive in order to make my major point clear: namely, that for Faulkner, the city of Memphis occupied a special relation to his own particular countryside, the countryside that provides the setting for nearly all his great novels. Beyond that, however, it is the larger cultural area which makes up the sub-region with which Faulkner was peculiarly concerned. If I had to put specific bounds on it, I would name the western tip of Kentucky, all of west Tennessee, and of course all of north Mississippi.

References to west Tennessee get into Faulkner's work more than occasionally. In his unfinished novel *Elmer,* the hero's shiftless family at one time lives in Paris, Tennessee. In his wonderful long story "The Bear," Isaac McCaslin, trying to find Tennie's Jim in order to give him his legacy, loses the trail at Jackson, Tennessee. The narrative of *Light in August* ends with the arrival of the truck, in which Lena and Byron Bunch have hitched a ride, in Saulsbury, Tennessee. Lena's happy ex-clamation, "My, my. A body does get around. Here we aint been com-ing from Alabama but two months, and now it's already Tennessee," constitutes the closing words of the novel.

In this subregion there is a white population principally English and Scotch-Irish in origin, along with a large black population. The popu-lation is heavily Protestant, with the Baptists the largest number and then, in something like descending order, Methodists, Presbyterians, and Episcopalians. Except in Memphis and a few other large centers, there are few Roman Catholics and Jews.

The Civil War hero for the whole subregion is Nathan Bedford For-rest, who was born in north Mississippi, is buried in Memphis, but whose fame extends into western Kentucky. In the stories of Irvin S. Cobb of Paducah, many of the characters are Confederate veterans who were immensely proud to have served under Forrest. Sixty and seventy years ago, Cobb was a very popular writer, and there is plenty of evidence that Faulkner knew his work and occasionally borrowed from it.

Joseph Blotner tells us about the historical basis for an incident Faulkner made use of in *The Unvanquished.* In 1863 the Seventh Ten-nessee Cavalry was retreating through the streets of Oxford, when a young woman rushed out to rebuke them for running away from the bluecoats. A captain in the regiment, one of General Forrest's sons, ad-mired the girl's pluck, vowed to himself that he would marry her, and after the war was over did return for her. The girl had left her mark on the window from which she had watched the column of soldiers—she scratched her name on the glass with the diamond in her ring. The incident obviously interested Faulkner, for twice he mentioned a girl's scratching her name on a window as she looks out on the street.

The little anecdote has a special interest for me also, for I have a grandfather who served in Company L of that same Seventh Tennessee Cavalry, and so I am happy to be able to find some personal connection with Faulkner's work even if my ancestor's relation to it is as anonymous as it is here, and portrays him and his companions engaged not in a victorious cavalry charge, but in grim and disconsolate retreat. But then one can't have everything.

In sum, Faulkner is clearly enough identified with the subregion that he chose to depict in his fiction. There is really no need to adduce more evidence. It is time to address other and finally more important issues, such as questions as these: What is the value, if there is any value at all, in reading such work as Faulkner has left us? Does it do any more than merely entertain us? Entertainment may have a high value of its own, but if that were all that a reading of Faulkner offered us, I would not think it was worth discussing. That is to say, that if the fiction provided by Faulkner was merely on a par with the more popular situation comedies or soap operas that make up the bulk of our television fare, or something as good as but not particularly better than the time-fillers and time-killers sold in airports, I would have no reason to consider the value of Faulkner's work.

The Scriptures tell us, "Thou canst not live by bread alone," nor by Crest toothpaste, Tide detergent, Skippy peanut butter, or Bayer aspirin. I make no judgment about the value of these products. At least one or two of them I use myself. The body has its just claims. But the inner man needs nourishment and remedies also. It needs to be *kept* reminded of the great virtues such as honor, truth telling, courage, responsibility, and of Saint Paul's triad of faith, hope, and charity.

The proclamation of these virtues is ultimately, of course, the responsibility of the church, and in the South many people do regularly attend church. But philosophy has a role to play too, and so do literature and the humanistic disciplines generally. They are at the least extremely valuable ancillary forces. They do things which religion in its more theological and liturgical roles cannot do.

Great literature, for example, can give us representations of human beings in action—in our various experiences of temptation as we feel the pressures of the times, the temptation to achieve success, to gain men's respect and women's love, to acquire wealth and power, to become a force in the community so that our names might even appear on the front page of the *Commercial Appeal* or the New York *Times*.

The best answer that I know to the question I have just raised was given some 2,500 years ago by Aristotle, the father of literary criticism. He argued that poetry (in which term he included drama and fiction) was more philosophical than history, for history gives an account of what happened, flukes, accidents, and all. Poetry, however, gives us a sense of what should have happened, the probable rather than the merely possible, of what events, given the circumstances, seem to be the inevitable result of those circumstances.

Yet poetry, like history, is concrete and particular in a way that philosophy is not. That is, poetry gives us more than abstractions and empty generalizations. Human beings want a sense of fact, of human beings in action, struggling against nature or with other human beings or with their own consciences.

We respond directly to this rich and dynamic world in which a Hamlet or a Lear struggles with himself and with a hostile world about him as we cannot directly respond to an abstract analysis of such concepts as duty, responsibility, and filial love and trust. In short, valuable and necessary as the normative sciences of logic and ethics are, we want to see ethics, for example, embodied in human beings, and ethical problems worked out in their actions.

On this point, however, a question might arise. Granted that any good author can provide us with intellectual and spiritual nourishment, is there anything more special that a writer from our own region provides for us? In short, why not simply read Shakespeare, Flaubert, or Dostoevsky? Why take the trouble to read Faulkner? It's a fair question. Let me begin my answer by saying that I would not want to discourage people from reading Shakespeare or any other great writer from the past. Nevertheless, a writer of our own time and place can make an important, special contribution. A great literary artist such as Faulkner helps the rest of the country and the rest of the world to understand us better. The region becomes humanized when a writer treats it in his work.

I have sojourned in New England for over thirty years, and I have taught Faulkner at Yale for many of those years and to hundreds of students, the great majority of whom were not from the South. To people whose only notion of our region and people is derived from newspaper headlines, radio and TV reports, sensational occurrences, and the distortions of political cartoons, the insights of a Faulkner or a Welty or a Warren or a Walker Percy are true revelations.

Yet even more important, I should say, is the revelation of our own region to ourselves. Every region needs its special spokesman to draw aside from the eyes of its people the veil of familiarity and routine everydayness, and to help them realize fully who they are.

Faulkner's set of novels and stories also tell us how we got here. His novels take us back to the time of the first settlements, when the Chickasaw Indians were still on the land and Memphis was a rough, outlying small river town. Other of his novels carry us on through the gathering clouds portending the coming of the Civil War, the war itself, and the dark Reconstruction period that followed. Novels dealing with a later time take us through World War I, with its disillusionments and the South's entrance into the modern world, and then on through the 1930s and 1940s, and into World War II.

The very landscape itself takes on a new dimension when we see it in the perspective of its history. What was before merely thin, raw, and matter of fact becomes rich with acquired depth, and gathers to itself remembered incidents out of its past. That is the way the literary artist sees a landscape or an old building or a historic battlefield, and since he possesses the artist's gift, he can help us also to perceive the scene through his eyes. In saying this, I do not mean falsifying illusions. I am saying that we can be taught to see what is truly there. For the great literary artists deal not in fraud but in truth. Such an artist makes us see with a gaze that does not stop at mere exteriors, but penetrates the inner meaning of a scene or event, and the meaning of events involves their history and how they came to be. So Faulkner, like any other great literary artist, provides us with scenes set against the backdrop of history. Because of it those scenes gain in energy and power over our minds and affections.

But I must not rely too much on generalizations. We need some concrete illustrations; we need to let Faulkner speak for himself.

Malcolm Cowley has written that "no other American writer takes such delight in the weather," by which Cowley doesn't mean that the weather Faulkner describes is always delightful. He means that Faulkner loved to savor the varying weather conditions and to try to describe them. Here are some of Cowley's selections, to which I have added a few of my own: Late summer in the pinewoods, "the hot still pinewiney silence of the August afternoon"; "the moonless September dusk, the trees along the road not rising soaring as trees should but squatting like huge fowl"; "the slow drizzle of November rain just above the ice point"; "those windless Mississippi December days which are a sort of Indian summer's Indian summer."

And here is a fine phrase describing the rife springtime of the mid-South: "the pollen wroiled chiaroscuro of spring"; in contrast to it, the sort of blank winter's day in the same region: "a gray day, of the color and texture of iron, one of those gray days of a plastic rigidity too dead to make or release snow." Here is a moonlit buggy ride over unpaved country roads in summertime: "night-time roads across the mooned or unmooned sleeping land, the mare's feet like silk in the dust"; in contrast to this lulled and slumbrous landscape, the September night skies as they appear to the leader of a lynching party after the victim has been killed: "There was no movement, no sound, not even an insect. The dark world seemed to lie stricken beneath the cold moon and the lidless stars." And lastly, a brief glance at turn-of-the-century Memphis, not yet come out of the horse-and-buggy age, as seen by an early motorist: "Suddenly before us was a wide tree-bordered and ordered boulevard with car tracks in the middle, and sure enough, there was the streetcar itself, the conductor and motorman just lowering the back trolley and raising the front one to turn it around and go back up to Main Street. . . . Besides the streetcars there were buggies and surreys—phaetons, traps, stanhopes, at least one victoria, the horses a little white-eyed at us but still collected; evidently Memphis horses were already used to automobiles."

More important, however, than these brilliant descriptions of climate and weather and countryside, village and city—and I could cite hundreds more—are Faulkner's dramatic scenes, often electric with excitement, which reveal personality and character in action. Here is a brief sampling.

My first is that of Drusilla Sartoris handing the pistols to her stepson. She is only eight years older than he and believes in the male code of honor and the code duello even more passionately than does any man of the time. She, along with the rest of the community, is confident that Bayard Sartoris will next morning avenge his father's death with a gun, and she means to hand him the gun as a sacred charge. Such, then, is the scene that greets Bayard's eyes when he steps inside his home. He meets no wailing widow in black, but a tearless young woman wearing a yellow ballgown. She says to Bayard:

> "Now let me look at you." She stood back, staring at me—the face tearless and exalted, the feverish eyes brilliant and voracious. "How beautiful you are: do you know it? How beautiful: young, to be permitted to kill, to be permitted vengeance, to take into your bare hands the fire of heaven that cast down Lucifer. No; I. I gave it to you; I put it into your hands; Oh you will thank me, you will remember me when I am dead and you are an old man saying to himself, 'I have tasted all things.' It will be the right hand, won't it?" She moved; she had taken my right hand which still held one of the pistols before I knew what she was about to do; she had bent and kissed it before I comprehended why she took it.

Pitched in a very different tonality is Dilsey's colloquy with her daughter Frony. Benjy is the retarded son of the Compson family. He is now thirty-three years old but has the mentality of a three-year-old child. Benjy's mother is ashamed of her son and to all of her children proves to be a whining, self-pitying, neurotic mother. Such true mother as the Compson children have they find in Dilsey, the kindly and resolute black servant who tries in vain to hold the Compson family together. On Easter Sunday, Dilsey takes Benjy to her own church with her, though her daughter Frony remonstrates with her for doing so.

> "I wish you wouldn't keep on bringin him to Church, mammy," Frony said. "Folks talkin."
>
> "What folks," Dilsey said.
>
> "I hears em," Frony said.
>
> "And I know what kind of folks," Dilsey said. "Trash white folks. Dat's who it is. Thinks he not good for white church, but nigger church aint good enough for him."
>
> "Dey talks jes de same," Frony said.
>
> "Then you send um to me," Dilsey said. "Tell um de good Lawd dont keer whether he smart er not. Dont nobody but white trash keer dat."

On this point Dilsey is as sound in her theology as she is warm and compassionate in her feelings. Fortunately for most of us, one does

not have to make a satisfactory IQ score to get into heaven. For orthodox Christianity, every soul, including that of a retarded person, is pre-
cious and has infinite worth.

My third example is one of heroic action and illustrates Faulkner's
ability to render a scene of violent action with wonderful vividness. It
describes the death of Old Ben, the bear that has been hunted annually
for years. He has seemed invulnerable, but finally the great hunting
dog named Lion brings him to bay, and Boon Hogganbeck, who is a
notoriously bad shot with a gun, throws his gun away and trusts to his
knife alone.

> This time the bear didn't strike [Lion] down. It caught the dog in both
> arms, almost loverlike, and they both went down. [Ike] was off the mule
> now. He drew back both hammers of the gun but he could see nothing but
> moiling spotted houndbodies until the bear surged up again. Boon was
> yelling something, he could not tell what; he could see Lion still clinging to
> the bear's throat and he saw the bear, half erect, strike one of the hounds
> with one paw and hurl it five or six feet and then, rising and rising as
> though it would never stop, stand erect again and begin to rake at Lion's
> belly with its forepaws. Then Boon was running. The boy saw the gleam of
> the blade in his hand and watched him leap among the hounds, hurdling
> them, kicking them aside as he ran, and fling himself astride the bear as he
> had hurled himself onto the mule, his legs locked around the bear's belly,
> his left arm under the bear's throat where Lion clung, and the glint of the
> knife as it rose and fell.
>
> It fell just once. For an instant they almost resembled a piece of statuary:
> the clinging dog, the bear, the man astride its back, working and probing
> the buried blade. Then they went down, pulled over backward by Boon's
> weight, Boon underneath. It was the bear's back which reappeared first but
> at once Boon was astride it again. He had never released the knife and again
> the boy saw the almost infinitesimal movement of his arm and shoulder as he
> probed and sought; then the bear surged erect, raising with it the man and
> the dog too, and turned and still carrying the man and the dog it took two or
> three steps toward the woods on his hind feet as a man would have walked
> and crashed down. It didn't collapse, crumple. It fell all of a piece, as a tree
> falls, so that all three of them, man dog and bear, seemed to bounce once.

I have given two examples of high drama and one in a lower key but
resonant with effective drama too, this time with tragic overtones. My

fourth and last example is in the comic mode. The incident I mean to present, from a novel called *The Hamlet,* tells of how a poor white farmer, Ab Snopes, is beaten in some very complicated horse trading by the redoubtable Pat Stamper of west Tennessee. Faulkner describes Stamper as a "heavy man with a stomach and a broad pale Stetson hat and eyes the color of a new axe blade."

Stamper makes his trading rounds accompanied by a black assistant who is a veritable magician in transforming the appearance of horses. He feeds them special drugs or dyes their hides a different color or plumps them out by inserting a bicycle tire valve under their hides and actually pumping them up. I remember when I was a child in Tennessee that the Gypsies were said sometimes to have practiced this last trick. Evidently Faulkner had heard the yarn too, and makes it one of Pat Stamper's tricks.

V. K. Ratliff was only a boy at the time of the Snopes-Stamper encounter, and accompanied Ab when he drove into town to take on Stamper. It is Ratliff who relates the story: the initial sparring, the actual trading, and then its aftermath. Ab had driven into town with a horse and a mule hitched to his wagon. He trades his oddly assorted team for a couple of mules. As Ratliff tells the story—though I quote only a part of it—at the beginning those mules looked all right: "They looked like two ordinary, not extra good mules you might see in a hundred wagons on the road." Still their jerky motions are a bit peculiar. Ab finally gets them straightened out and pulling together.

> They moved at the same time for the first time in their lives, or for the first time since Ab owned them anyway, and here we come swurging up that hill and into the Square like a roach up a drainpipe, with the wagon on two wheels and Ab sawing at the reins and saying "Hell fire, hell fire" and folks, ladies and children mostly, scattering and screeching and Ab just managed to swing them into the alley behind Cain's store and stopped them by locking our nigh wheel with another wagon's and the other team (they was hitched) holp to put the brakes on. So it was a good crowd by then, helping us to get untangled, and Ab led our team over to Cain's back door and tied them snubbed up close to a post, with folks still coming up and saying "It's that team of Stamper's," and Ab breathing hard now and looking a right smart less easy in the face and most all-fired watchful. "Come on," he says. "Let's get that damn [cream] separator and get out of here."

So we went in and give Cain Miz Snopes's rag and he counted the twenty-four sixty-eight and we got the separator and started back to the wagon, to where we had left it. Because it was still there; the wagon wasn't the trouble. In fact, it was too much wagon. I mind how I could see the bed and the tops of the wheels where Ab had brought it up close against the loading platform and I could see the folks from the waist up standing in the alley, twice or three times as many of them now, and I was thinking how it was too much wagon and too much folks; it was like one of these here pictures that have printed under them, *What's wrong with this picture?* and then Ab begun to say "Hell fire, hell fire" and begun to run, still toting his end of the separator, up to the edge of the platform where we could see under it. The mules was all right too. They was laying down. Ab had snubbed them up pretty close to the same post, with the same line through both bits, and now they looked exactly like two fellows that had done hung themselves in one of these here suicide packs, with their heads snubbed up together and pointing straight up and their tongues hanging out and their eyes popping and their necks stretched about four foot and their legs doubled back under them like shot rabbits until Ab jumped down and cut them down with his pocket knife. A artist. [Stamper's black assistant] had give them just exactly to the inch of whatever it was to get them to town and off the square before it played out.

In scenes such as these, we have vivid and dramatic portrayals of human beings, acting out their emotions and making their choices and decisions, some serious, some comic. The works of Faulkner are filled with such scenes.

In conclusion, let me point out that the South, and this particular subregion of the South, has been most fortunate in possessing an interpreter with Faulkner's stature. He can do for this region what Robert Burns and Sir Walter Scott did for Scotland in the early nineteenth century, or what William Butler Yeats and James Joyce did for Ireland in the twentieth. He constitutes a magnificent cultural resource. I hope that for pleasure and for a deeper understanding of this region, readers will turn to his works again and again.

Faulkner's
"Motherless" Children

The world created by Faulkner is vast and fantastically rich in characters and dramatic situations. It is also a world which, in spite of various marvelous and unlikely happenings, is convincingly lifelike—so much so that the reader is sometimes tempted to forget that it is finally an imaginary world, one created by William Faulkner.

It was, to be sure, made out of something. Faulkner never pretended to be, like the Almighty God, able to create *ex nihilo*. Indeed, we know where the materials came from: in great part from William Faulkner's experience through a particular tract of time in a particular cultural environment.

As is probably clear, I am not of the newly arisen group of critics who seem to be saying that literature refers to nothing outside itself—is only self-referential, a mere shadow play of words with other words. On the contrary, I believe that Faulkner's fiction can tell us something about the South during the first half of the twentieth century and about the human beings to be found there. I believe that we can learn something not only about William Faulkner but also about ourselves.

So I am tempted, like most of us, to mistake some of his fictional characters for truly flesh-and-blood people, and to treat them as if they were. Nevertheless, I shall try to keep clearly in mind that Faulkner's purpose is not to conduct a guided tour through the South. He is not

Given as a lecture at the 1984 Faulkner Conference at Wayne State University, Detroit, and originally published in slightly different form in *William Faulkner: Materials, Studies, and Criticism,* VII (April, 1984).

a sociologist or a psychoanalyst or a political scientist. He is neither lecturing us nor preaching to us. Rather, he is rendering experiences through imagined situations in terms of what is essentially the dramatic mode; that is to say, he is allowing us to observe human beings in interaction. Sometimes, his method departs from that of the quite objective onlooker and so takes us into the minds of his characters. But even here, good artist that he is, he does not dictate to his reader what conclusions that reader ought to draw.

But enough of generalizations. It's time that I get down to particular cases and to specific issues. The special case with which I shall be concerned is what seems to be Faulkner's preoccupation with men and women who at an early age have lost their mothers by death or whose living mothers have in effect abandoned them.

Once you turn your attention to this matter, you wonder why you had not noticed it before. Yet it was only the other day that the sheer number of Faulkner's motherless characters struck me forcefully.

Let me offer some examples. In *Light in August,* there are three important characters who are all "motherless": Joe Christmas, Gail Hightower, and Lena Grove. In *Go Down, Moses,* McCaslin Edmonds, whom most readers of Faulkner will remember as Old Cass, lost his father early and his mother earlier still. He was brought up by his maternal uncles. In *The Unvanquished,* Bayard Sartoris (to be known later as "Old" Bayard) has been rendered motherless at least by the age of thirteen. In *Flags in the Dust* (and in its shortened version, *Sartoris*), "Young" Bayard and his twin John are not the sons but the grandsons of Old Bayard. Their father had died in 1901 when the twins were four years old. Their mother lived long enough to spoil them rotten, according to Miss Jenny, their great-aunt, but when the action of the novel begins, their mother has been long dead. Young Bayard never refers to her.

In the same novel, Horace and his sister Narcissa Benbow have, the novel implies, been orphaned for a long time. Also in the novel we find the McCallums, a father and his six sons who lead a healthy, almost pioneer life far from town in a completely masculine household. The only female presence is that of Mandy, the old black woman who cooks for them.

In Faulkner's first novel, *Soldiers' Pay,* three important characters lack mothers: Donald Mahon, Emmy, and Januarius Jones. In "A Rose for

Emily," Faulkner's first published story, Miss Emily had lost her mother, presumably very early. We hear a great deal about her father and his influence on her early life, but not one word about her mother.

In *The Wild Palms,* a mother abandons her husband and little girls to elope with a young man with whom she is desperately in love. In *Pylon,* a mother gives up her little son to his paternal grandparents. In *Requiem for a Nun,* another mother is on the point of abandoning her two small children in order to elope with her lover. She is prevented from doing so by the death of the infant, a circumstance that brings her back to her moral senses.

There are other motherless children in Faulkner's stories and novels. Rather than continue with this catalogue, however, I want to address the question of why Faulkner chose to give us so many characters who lack mothers. Yet I must say that I shall offer no simple answer. And what answers I shall suggest will have to wait until we have examined more of the evidence. But I can mention here and now some answers that I do not mean to offer.

First, I will not propose a psychoanalytic explanation and, by doing so, argue that the answer lies in some predisposition of Faulkner's own psyche, some emotional quirk that kept him obsessed with a personal sense of loss. I pretend to no competency in this field. Moreover, such accounts usually end by telling us more about the author's psyche than about the meaning of his work. Surely, it is too simple to say that a knowledge of a writer's psyche, even if we possess it, ever fully accounts for what his imagination produces.

I have a comment to make before leaving this topic: The agreed-upon interpretation is that Faulkner had a strong-willed and dominant mother and a weak and ineffectual father. This is the gist of a number of biographical accounts. In the past we have been told that this family situation often produces a homosexual son. But Faulkner, whatever he was, was not that, nor can I find any such characters in his fiction. In his novels he does give us several examples of the dominant mother and the weak father; but he also wrote many more in which the mother is absent or weak. And he also wrote a few in which the father and mother have achieved something like an optimum balance and harmony. The evidence of Faulkner's stories and novels seems to indicate that he was not fixated on one situation, but could write with plausibility and conviction on the whole range of possible parental relationships.

Nor am I going to argue that his devotion to his mother, whom, we are told, every day that he was in Oxford he punctiliously visited, actually concealed a secret desire to be rid of such an emotional burden, and that his longing to be free expressed itself in male characters who bore no such burden because the possibly possessive mother lay safely in her grave. For all I know, Faulkner may have consciously or unconsciously longed to be rid of his sense of obligation to his mother. I suppose that once in a while any dutiful son or daughter could chafe under this tie. But how little this fact—if indeed it is fact—tells us about characters as diverse as Isaac McCaslin, Joe Christmas, and young Bayard Sartoris. In order to illustrate how differently they used their freedom from this emotional bond, let me cite their careers: that of the desperately obsessed Joe Christmas, who longs to know who and what he is; or that of Isaac McCaslin, who is trying to imitate Christ; or that of Young Bayard, who strives in vain to find some action in which he can fulfill himself.

But in rejecting such explanations, I trust that I will not fall into some other simplistic solution that ignores the complexities of the problem. What I propose to do is to approach the problem in quite other terms: not to ask what quirk in Faulkner's own psychic life might have prompted him to write so frequently about motherless children, but the possible significance the fact holds for the story or novel in which such a character is found. In short, what I shall be asking is what artistic need is accounted for by the circumstance in question, not what psychic urge, conscious or unconscious in Faulkner, his orphaned characters satisfy.

Yet one further preliminary word: May not the problem I have raised be a bogus problem? Why should a novelist ever bother about whether his characters have living mothers or not? Many writers never do. Hemingway, for example, hardly ever writes about such characters. True enough, but Faulkner generally does take the family seriously. In the culture that provided him with his materials, the family is very important. Moreover, again and again Faulkner focuses upon the nurture and development of his characters—Donald Mahon, Ike McCaslin, Joe Christmas, the two Bayard Sartorises, Miss Zilphia Gant, Thomas Sutpen, and on and on. We cannot simply brush the problem aside as being no problem at all.

Let us consider one or two concrete instances. In "A Rose for Emily," Faulkner wanted to isolate Miss Emily Grierson almost completely and to throw her back on her own resources. The early loss of a girl's mother is an obvious way of heightening her loneliness and stressing her father's power over her.

In *Soldiers' Pay,* Faulkner's purpose in presenting three of his characters as virtually, if not absolutely, motherless is quite different. Donald Mahon is described again and again as a faun; Emmy as a nymph; and Januarius Jones as a yellow-eyed, lecherous satyr. In Greek mythology very little is ever said about the parentage of such beings. It would be almost as embarrassing for a nymph to have a mother as for a faun to have a mother-in-law. In any case, the modern world has no room for an innocent paganism, though perhaps more than enough for satyrs. Donald and Emmy come to grief; the unspeakable Jones, that perversion of an innocent paganism, ends up getting his way with Emmy.

In *Flags in the Dust,* Faulkner apparently has still another reason for depriving young Bayard Sartoris of his parents and Narcissa and Horace Benbow of theirs. He wants to present a direct juxtaposition of the World War I generation with a generation that had experienced the Civil War. Old Bayard, the grandfather, knows who he is and how a man of honor ought to act. Young Bayard, who has grown up in his grandfather's house, is, by contrast, baffled, restless, and even desperate. We find a comparable pattern in Narcissa's associations with Aunt Jenny Du Pre, Old Bayard's aunt. Miss Jenny is a lady; Narcissa, in her self-absorption, is simply "respectable," a very low category in Faulkner's estimation.

In *Sanctuary* we learn that seventeen-year-old Temple Drake had lost her mother; though *how* early in her life is not disclosed, I should think it was quite early. Even the memory of her mother is never invoked in the novel. As Temple goes through her horrifying experience she never seems to think of her mother at all, though in her unbelief at what is happening to her, she does say, "My father is a judge," perhaps as a proof that she is merely dreaming. The daughter of a judge simply could not be treated in this manner.

Had Temple experienced a mother's care and guidance, would she have been a different person and would her story have had a different conclusion? I shall not hazard a guess, and I take it that Faulkner made no attempt to draw any such conclusion. Whether a real mother would have made a difference would likely have depended upon what kind of woman the mother was. Moreover, Faulkner was wise enough to know that men and women who have sensible and loving mothers often come to grief.

Thus, in *The Wild Palms,* Harry Wilbourne tries to support himself and the woman with whom he eloped. He cranks out for the confessions magazines stories that begin "If I had only had a mother's love to guide me on that fatal day. . . ." Here speaks Faulkner the realist and the ironist. He harbored no illusions about the invincible power of a mother's love.

Faulkner was not obsessed with the plight of the motherless child. He could and did write about children who had strong and powerful mothers. Yet even there the consequences could be mixed. In *As I Lay Dying,* for example, Addie Bundren is a woman married to a shiftless and pusillanimous husband. Three of her four sons love her intensely, though each in his own way: Vardaman, with a young child's complete dependence; Cash, with a quiet, unimpassioned loyalty; Jewel, with a burning though almost inarticulate ardor. Addie's daughter too grieves over her dying mother. But the fourth son, Darl? What of him? His attitude is complex. I shall not try to analyze it here. But in any case the strong-willed mother could not save her children from her husband Anse's selfish calculations—at least, as the novel concludes, she has not saved them. When the wagonful of Bundrens heads home, minus Darl and Addie, it bears in Addie's place the duck-shaped woman whom Anse has just married, not a very promising stepmother.

Miss Zilphia Gant, in the story of that title, is another woman who has experienced the blessing (or perhaps it is the curse) of a strong-willed mother. Zilphia knows little of her father, for her mother early disposes of her erring husband by drilling him with a few competently aimed pistol shots.

Miss Zilphia's story does have a quasi-happy ending, though it is a rather bizarre one and certainly does not involve a shower of rice and the start of a joyous honeymoon. Faulkner simply has her repeat her mother's role as the strong-minded woman bringing up a young girl. The child is not Zilphia's daughter but the orphaned child of Zilphia's husband; and so Zilphia—she is Miss Zilphia to the end—escapes the trials of a wife but is allowed to revel in the joys of untrammeled motherhood.

I think it would be difficult to find in either of these examples I have mentioned any reflections of the family life that Faulkner himself experienced as a child and youth. Faulkner's strong-minded mother, wedded to an ineffectual husband, does not bear any close resemblance to either Addie Bundren or Mrs. Gant. Some readers, I would expect, would see something of Faulkner in Darl, Addie's artistic, introspective son. Perhaps. But I would find something of Faulkner in Jewel as well. You can, of course, by forcing the evidence a little here and there, prove almost anything that you choose to prove. That's just the difficulty: every artist puts something of himself into every one of his characters. I am sure that Shakespeare put a little of himself even into the villainous Iago. In any case, Faulkner could write well about families with a strong-minded mother as well as about families without any mother at all.

Did he ever write about families in which there was balance between the mother and the father? He certainly did. That is the impression that one gets from reading *Intruder in the Dust*. Chick Mallison, the young hero of the novel, grows up in a healthy family. Perhaps Chick would have achieved his moral growth even in another environment; but then perhaps he would not have done so. One thinks also of *The Reivers*, which depicts the moral growth of the boy Lucius Priest. Again, there is a happy family relationship and, perhaps not coincidentally, a happy ending to the novel.

It can be objected that in neither of these novels does Faulkner emphasize the mother and father; instead, attention is focused on the adventures and the development of their son. But it is not hard to come up with a rejoinder to such an objection. Tolstoy gave it long ago when he said happy families are all alike, which, translated into the novelist's terms, means that in such situations, there is not much to say or that one needs to say about the family environment. Novelists proverbially want to deal with the problematic relationships. It is in these that a possibility of excitement and drama lies.

So let us return to those novels in which the mother's presence is lacking or else viciously negative. These novels will, not surprisingly, include those which, by common account, are Faulkner's greatest.

With reference to one of these, however, space allows me to do little more than mention it. I refer to *Go Down, Moses*. The central figure of this novel, Isaac McCaslin, was the child of his father's old age, and the father was dead by the time Isaac was ten years old. The evidence would suggest that Isaac's mother had died earlier. She simply does not figure at all in the story of Isaac's growing up. One is tempted to speculate about how much this early loss of a mother may have had to do with Isaac's unhappy and short-lived marriage, with his refusal to inherit his patrimony, and with his long life as a man who was "uncle to half a county and father to no one." But I shall have to leave the problem at precisely this point.

I want to consider *The Sound and the Fury* and *Light in August*. In *The Sound and the Fury* the Compson children have a living mother, but as a mother she is a disaster. She poisons the whole household. She is bitterly ashamed of Benjy, the retarded son. For mothering, he has to depend on his sister Caddy and on Dilsey, the kindly black servant. Mrs. Compson has spoiled rotten the insufferable Jason, the son on whom she dotes. She badly mishandles her daughter Caddy. A typical instance is her donning mourning apparel when she learns that Caddy has allowed a boy to kiss her.

One turns to her son Quentin for the most explicit statement of the damage that Mrs. Compson has wrought. On the day on which he commits suicide, he is saying to himself: *"Done in Mother's mind, though. Finished. Finished. Then we were all poisoned,"* and even more poignantly, he tells himself, *"If I could say Mother. Mother."* It may be better to have no mother at all than a mother who is thoroughly negative.

Am I letting Mr. Compson off too lightly? Perhaps I am. The father who occupies Quentin's thoughts on his last day is a defeated, world-weary man, one who relies even more on bourbon whiskey than on his stoic philosophy to get him through his unhappy life. The counsel that he gives Quentin hardly suffices. It certainly does not prevent Quentin's suicide—it rather encourages it. In fairness to Mr. Compson, however, one has to remember that the testimony of Quentin on this day in which he has fully accepted his own defeat is perhaps somewhat skewed. The few glimpses that we get of Mr. Compson in Benjy's confused mind, and from Dilsey, and from some remarks of Caddy's as remembered by Quentin give a rather different impression. Furthermore, if it is fair to take into account what we learn of Mr. Compson in *Absalom, Absalom!* and in "That Evening Sun," that better impression is amply confirmed.

I grant that a father who was wiser and stronger than Mr. Compson might have done more to prevent the wreck of his family. Nevertheless, I am considering the roles of the mother and the motherless child, and so I believe that I may be forgiven for introducing *The Sound and the Fury* as another bit of prime evidence of the plight of Faulkner's motherless children. Yet one should not leave off discussing this novel without mentioning the plight of the most damaged of all Faulkner's motherless children. I have in mind, of course, the girl Quentin, Caddy's child, whom she made the sad mistake of leaving to grow up in the poisoned atmosphere of the Compson household. Dilsey does the best she can for the girl, and Caddy faithfully sends ample bank checks to support her. But neither Dilsey nor her faraway mother can save the girl Quentin.

In *Light in August* we have two males that count as motherless children. Joe Christmas is clearly so. His young mother had died either in giving birth to him or only a few hours after. As for Gail Hightower, his mother died before he had reached the age of eight. She was in any case an invalid. We learn that "if on the day of her death [Gail] had been told that he had ever seen her otherwise than in bed, he would not have believed it." Gail's father was a reserved man, many years older than his little son and always remote from him. So, as Faulkner puts it, the "son grew to manhood among phantoms, and side by side with a ghost. The phantoms were his father, his mother, and an old Negro woman." Again, I quote Faulkner's very words: "With this phantom [the old Negro servant woman] the child talked about the ghost." The ghost was Gail's grandfather, a Confederate cavalryman, who became the child's heroic ideal. The image of the cavalryman, galloping to his death, comes to dominate Hightower's life and to induce him to live in a dream of the past.

So the adult Hightower becomes a dreamer, a passive observer of the activity around him. The other motherless child in the novel, Joe Christmas, takes an exactly opposite course. He is impelled into action—even violent action—in his urgent quest to discover who he really is. He has no way of knowing. When he is a few months old, his crazed grandfather leaves him on the doorstep of a Memphis orphanage. Here Joe spends his childhood.

If anyone doubts the importance that Faulkner placed on the relation of a child to its mother, let him read Faulkner's poignant rendering of a small and apparently unimportant episode when Joe was three years old. It is worth quoting in full.

> One day there was missing from among them a girl of twelve named Alice. He had liked her, enough to let her mother him a little; perhaps because of it. And so to him she was as mature, almost as large in size, as the adult women who ordered his eating and washing and sleeping, with the difference that she was not and never would be his enemy. One night she waked him. She was telling him goodbye but he did not know it. He was sleepy and a little annoyed, never full awake, suffering her because she had always tried to be good to him. He didn't know that she was crying because he did not know that grown people cried, and by the time he learned that, memory had forgotten her. He went back into sleep while still suffering her, and the next morning she was gone. Vanished, no trace of her left, not even a garment, the very bed in which she had slept already occupied by a new boy. He never did know where she went to.

One feels that if Joe had received more such tenderness early, perhaps he would not have come to look upon womankind with suspicion and even fear, would not have come to regard all adult women as his enemies. As it was, however, one encounter after another with women confirmed the child's early sense of them as enemies.

Remember the episode of Joe's eating the dietician's toothpaste and the misunderstanding on the part of the woman as well as the child; his foster mother, who put him off by her awkward attempts to mother him and to protect him from his stern Calvinistic foster father; his betrayal by his first love, Bobbie, the part-time waitress and part-time prostitute; and his strange affair with Joanna Burden, who became his mistress and then later, having become penitent, tries to save Joe's soul. When she began to pray over him, she signed her death warrant. His fear and hatred of women, those creatures who cannot be trusted, who refuse to keep the rules, who play upon one's emotions to get their way—all his pent-up rage at woman's nature bursts forth and Joe decapitates her and flees into the woods.

Yet more than perverted fear of the feminine principle is involved. Early in Joe's life there had been insinuated the suspicion that he might be a child of mixed racial heritage. Joe himself has no real evidence to go on. In a conversation with Joanna Burden he confides that he thinks that one of his parents was a Negro. But when Joanna asks him how he knows it, Joe says frankly, "I don't know it," and I believe that Faulkner means for us to accept his statement as the truth.

Joe has no difficulty in passing for a white man. No one ever questions his white status until Joe himself raises the issue. Nevertheless, the suspicion for a long time rankles in Joe's mind. He needs to tell others about it, perhaps as a test of their feelings toward him: thus he voices his suspicion not only to Joanna but to Bobbie Allen and to the wretched Joe Brown, his partner in his bootlegging business.

Joe's concern about his race, even if it has no factual basis, is important to him. For three years he had tried living among the blacks as a black man. But he found no more satisfactory life among the black community than the white. He remained prickly on the whole subject of race. Once he told a white prostitute that he was a black man and when she accepted the fact with perfect equanimity, he nearly beat her to death.

If anyone feels that Joe's conduct is really incomprehensible behavior, I could call his attention to a story that appeared in the New York *Times* for June 6, 1983. A Mr. Banks had been accused of the murder of thirteen people, including three white women with whom he had been living. Banks was himself the child of a white mother and a black father. Banks's mother and one of his close associates said that he "suffered a sense of alienation because of his mixed parentage." The associate also said that Banks "seethed with resentment against the two races whose heritages he shared."

Now the cases of Joe Christmas and the man in the *Times* account are not identical. My point is simply that mixed parentage, whether actual or simply a matter of belief, can generate a sense of alienation and a resentment against both races. In *Light in August,* Faulkner has envisaged human reactions which can occur in fact.

What, however, has this matter of mixed blood to do with Joe's suspicion of the feminine principle? Evidently a good deal, at least in Faulkner's account of the character of Joe Christmas. Earlier in the evening of the night on which Joe killed his former mistress, he is wandering rather aimlessly through the town of Jefferson. He finds himself in the Negro quarter of town. Here is what Faulkner writes: "On all sides, even within him, the bodiless fecundmellow voices of negro women murmured. It was as though he and all other manshaped life about him had returned to the lightless hot wet primogenitive Female.

He began to run, glaring, his teeth glaring, his inbreath cold on his dry teeth and lips, toward the next street lamp." Joe does associate the blacks with a feminine quality—perhaps because he sees black people as closer to nature and its instinctual life than are white people, just as he sees women as closer to nature than men are.

Joe then rushes away from the black quarter into the white part of town. On this hot summer night the white people are here and there sitting "on a lighted veranda . . . , the white faces intent and sharp in the light, the bare arms of the women glaring smooth and white above the trivial cards." Nothing "fecundmellow" here. Even the faces of the white women seem to Joe "intent and sharp." These two contrasting vignettes well express Joe's inability to be at ease with either the white or the black community.

Joe indeed is an incarnation of the masculine principle in its most nakedly aggressive form. He is at odds with the human community, with womankind, and with nature itself. Yet *incarnation* is not the accurate word here. Joe's perverted status does not come from his birth but from his nurture. As someone aptly characterized him years ago, he is the perfect example of completely institutionalized man. His earliest formative years were spent in a rather grim orphanage, and if, at the end, he had been content to abide by his lawyer's plea bargaining, he would have closed his days in an even more grim prison.

Thomas Sutpen is another stark manifestation of sheer masculinity. The God whom he worships is much the same God that Joe Christmas worships and would imitate: a God of justice, not of mercy. Pity, emotional appeals for mitigation or for merciful exemptions are scorned. Sutpen asks favor of nobody, human or divine. He counts solely on his own sound calculation, thorough performance, and invincible determination to see him through. Unlike Joe, he has no fear of the feminine principle. He simply disregards it.

Sutpen, one feels, never learns the truth about himself or about reality. He never stops trying and never loses confidence in himself. Thus he suffers his fate blindly if somehow heroically.

His children are another story. Poor Henry, his son, who is squeamish where his father is flintlike, who believes in honor, needs a role model, worships his friend, Charles Bon, and then feels that to protect his sister and to meet the demands of honor, he must kill that friend. Poor Henry. His life was cruelly wasted.

How much can this waste and misdirection be blamed upon the fact that his father was Thomas Sutpen and that his mother was a vapid, vain, and silly woman? Who can speak confidently in any such case? Nevertheless, one can feel that Henry was sent into the battle of life terribly handicapped. In some curious way, and in spite of vast differences, he reminds us of Quentin Compson. Perhaps there is a resemblance, and if so, it may account for Quentin's fascination with Henry Sutpen's life. His first and only sight of Henry as he lies on the yellowed sheets in an upstairs bedroom at Sutpen's Hundred, of Henry who had lived as an exile for nearly his whole life and, as he himself said, had come home to die—this vision burned itself into Quentin's brain. He obviously never can shake it off.

The life of Charles Bon, the son that Sutpen refused to recognize as his son, was as disastrous as Henry's. Quentin believed that all that Charles wanted was a word of recognition from his father, and failing to get it, though hoping that it would eventually come, he insisted on turning the screw tighter and tighter on his father and incidentally tightened it on Henry, who shot him dead at the very gates of Sutpen's Hundred. Charles Bon must have known Henry would have to kill him, but refused to alter his course of action. It seems that he actually yearned for his death.

We know little of Charles Bon's mother beyond Quentin's and Shreve's speculations about her. But we know a great deal about his father. If Faulkner depicted two mothers who abandoned their children, he provided in Thomas Sutpen a father who abandoned his sons.

Judith, however, was perhaps of all Sutpen's children the one that he injured most, and yet in a curious way, she was the child who most resembled him. She inherited his iron resolution, his staying power. But Judith possessed what her father entirely lacked, compassion and pity and love.

She is one of Faulkner's most admirable characters. She took care of her father after he had lost his fortune and fallen on evil days. She revered the memory of her dead fiancé, Charles Bon. She sought out and brought to Sutpen's Hundred her fiancé's common-law wife so that she might see her husband's grave. Later on, after this woman's death, Judith brought back to Sutpen's Hundred her child, Charles Bon's son, and, in spite of her dire poverty, reared the little fellow.

His name was Charles Étienne Saint-Valery Bon, and of Faulkner's motherless children, he perhaps suffered most of all from his orphaned state. He grew up as a lonely and bewildered child, the silken clothes he had known in New Orleans exchanged for a cotton shirt and over- alls, living in the company of two strange, rather taciturn women. But we must remember that Judith gave him the best she had.

I grant that had Judith had a loving mother and an affectionate fa- ther, and if the losses and disappointments of her life had not forced her into an almost grim stoicism, she might have given to little Charles the mothering for which he yearned but which she scarcely knew how to give.

Quentin Compson imagines a scene in which Judith begs Charles to address her as "Aunt Judith." She was in fact his half-aunt, though she did not know it. But the young man, out of some kind of pride, insists on calling her "Miss Judith," addressing her as the white woman who owns the plantation on which he finds himself and refusing any warmer term.

As I said, Quentin has simply imagined the scene. Nothing in the novel gives it a solid basis. But I trust Quentin's insight here and be- lieve that he understood Judith's character better than some of Faulk- ner's critical authorities have understood it.

Charles Étienne Bon is very much like Joe Christmas, who may have been his forerunner in Faulkner's imagination. Charles almost cer- tainly had some black ancestry; Joe, in my opinion, almost certainly did not. Yet both wondered about who they were in this white-domi- nated society with its racial caste system. That question to each of them was immensely important. Almost as important, I should say, is that both were also members of that large class of Faulkner's charac- ters—his motherless children.

Faulkner's Women
Light in August
and The Hamlet

Was Faulkner able to depict his women characters with insight and give them vitality? In my opinion, Faulkner portrays women with great skill. I would like to think that a great artist's comprehension transcends the boundaries of sex just as it transcends those of nationality. If only women can write well about women, then perhaps only men can write about men, only murderers can write well about murderers, only idiots, about idiots, and so on into absurdity. Surely the importance of the literary artist is that he can enter into all kinds of characters.

I can answer with much more confidence the question whether Faulkner regarded his women characters with admiration and/or compassion. Surely, he did. That was his own testimony as to his intentions, and I believe he succeeded in his actual literary performance.

I must admit, however, that Faulkner's early work provoked opinions to the contrary, some of which still persist. Faulkner was often accused of regarding women with hostility. They were instinctively wiser than men were, and their wisdom perhaps had a sinister side. They used their power over men for their own selfish ends. They were temptresses, daughters of Eve who were always offering to a simple-minded Adam the forbidden fruit.

Given as a lecture at the 1982 Gulf States Arts Association meeting in Gulfport, Miss.

Such accusers often played their trump card by pointing out that the only women for whom Faulkner showed obvious admiration were white-haired matriarchs. Thus, even in Japan, Faulkner was asked whether he had not shown in his fiction a fear and hostility toward young nubile women. Now there is no doubt that Faulkner's characters are responsive to the sexual attraction of women, and the evidence indicates that so was their creator. He had great respect for the power—for both good and evil—of the sexual urge. But I refuse to concede that Faulkner was hostile to women as such. That he was fascinated by women, good and bad, should be plain enough to any sensitive reader of his fiction, and that is the real test.

Faulkner told one inquirer that he found women simply wonderful; he liked to write about them. To another inquirer about his attitude toward women, he cited his admiration for Lena Grove. "I wrote her story," Faulkner said, "out of my admiration for women, for the courage and endurance of women." I believe him, for I believe that a reading of his fiction bears this out. Furthermore, Lena Grove was not an elderly matriarch with aristocratic manners. She was a simple farm girl, clearly of marriageable age, though unmarried when her story begins.

I mean to discuss the women characters in Faulkner's *Light in August,* published in 1932, and some of those in *The Hamlet,* published in 1940. These novels provide a rather full range of female types: strong-minded women, some of heroic proportions; women who are cowed and victimized by their husbands; women who are in the full bloom of their first beauty; and women who are beaten down after a life of heavy toil. In these two novels, there is at least one example of perfect love, a women who loves her husband passionately and whose love is fully returned by her husband; and, at the other end of the scale, there is a common prostitute. Yet even the prostitute, Bobbie Allen, I would point out, is depicted with some compassion—not with either clinical detachment or bitter contempt.

The two novels contain as their heroines two of Faulkner's so-called earth goddesses, Lena Grove and Eula Varner. The term *earth goddess,* however, is not wholly accurate. True, both young women embody to an intense degree the vitality of nature. Lena can fairly be called an earth goddess, for she is truly of the earth, earthy. Although she is not grubby or coarse, she does respond, apparently effortlessly, to the natural rhythms of growth and development to which the earth itself responds. If in a sense she is the force that harbors the seed and brings the germinating organism to perfection, if she is the sexual force renewing and sustaining the animate world, she is not at all the sexual temptress using lures and wiles.

There is not the slightest hint that she ever strove to attract the wretched weakling who got her with child, or that later on she makes the slightest effort to capture the love of Byron Bunch. It is more a matter of her simply trusting her natural instincts to carry her to a complete sexual fulfillment in the birth of her child. Her charm is her complete freedom from guile or calculation. She resembles "the lilies of the field, . . . they toil not, neither do they spin," or, we could say, she is like "the fowls of the air [which] sow not, neither do they reap, nor gather into barns." It is Lena's simplicity and her boundless faith that all will finally be well that carry her through.

Faulkner does not, of course, make the mistake of trying to pass her off as either a saint or a charmingly instinctive animal. He provides the little touches that render her human and feminine—as when, eating sardines, she congratulates herself that she eats like a lady; or her moments of coquetry with her ardent but tongue-tied lover, Byron Bunch.

Bunch had at first sight fallen in love with this obviously pregnant girl and had, like the perfect knight, cared for her and protected her through her lying-in and the birth of her child. At the end of the novel he is still accompanying her on a wild-goose chase after the child's father, who obviously has no intention of marrying her and has fled the country.

After some three weeks of travel, Byron is sore beset. Lena seems to have no intention of giving up the fruitless pursuit of her seducer and marrying her true lover, who has manifested his utter devotion to her in every way. At last Byron tears himself away from Lena, but next day rushes back in time to rejoin her as she prepares to go on. Byron mutters by way of explanation: "I done come too far now. I be dog if I'm going to quit now."

To which Lena coolly replies: "Aint nobody never said for you to quit." This is as much encouragement as she doles out to her unhappy lover, and this is what I mean by her coquetry. But as we lay down the novel, we realize that her drop of encouragement will be enough—that

Lena will eventually give up her absurd search, marry her faithful lover, and settle down.

If Lena is of the earth, earthy, almost as "natural" as nature itself, Faulkner's other earth goddess, Eula Varner, is hardly of this earth at all. She is depicted almost as a fertility goddess. She is intensely female and casts a spell over any man who views her. Here is Faulkner's initial description of her:

> She was the last of the sixteen children, the baby, though she had overtaken and passed her mother in height in her tenth year. Now, though not yet thirteen years old, she was already bigger than most grown women and even her breasts were no longer the little, hard, fiercely-pointed cones of puberty or even maidenhood. On the contrary, her entire appearance suggested some symbology out of the old Dionysi[a]c times—honey in sunlight and bursting grapes, the writhen bleeding of the crushed fecundated vine beneath the hard rapacious trampling goat-hoof. She seemed to be not a living integer of her contemporary scene, but rather to exist in a teeming vacuum in which her days followed one another as though behind soundproof glass, where she seemed to listen in sullen bemusement, with a weary wisdom heired of all mammalian maturity, to the enlarging of her own organs.

This is Faulkner's purple prose at its most purple. He writes with all the stops pulled out. But it is effective. In passages such as this—and there are many of them in *The Hamlet*—Faulkner succeeds in creating the sense that Eula is a pagan goddess, one fit to follow in the train of the old Greek god Dionysus. Symbolically, she too, like Lena, signifies the vitality and power of the forces of nature, but in her the natural forces are etherialized. Eula is raised above the merely human. It is by the barest minimum that Faulkner manages to keep her credibly human.

Like Lena, Eula is no temptress. She seems utterly oblivious to the commotion she creates among the men. She is quite indifferent to her horde of suitors. They bore her, and she suffers their attentions only, it seems, because such is expected of any young woman of her age.

It is only when a young man from town, Hoake McCarron, discovers her, courts her, and defeats his rivals that she becomes sexually awakened. He takes her for long buggy rides through the dreaming countryside on summer nights. One night, Eula and her suitor meet a gang of his rivals at the ford across the river, waiting in ambush. Hoake fights off his assailants, and Eula, using the heavy stock of the buggy whip, joins in the fight. Hoake suffers a broken arm, and Eula drives him back to the Varner house long past midnight. For the first time this indolent, passive beauty, uninterested in and even contemptuous of men, has awakened to sex through the primitive emotions aroused during the fight at the ford, and so she takes Hoake to bed with her, though she has to support his body—his arm is broken—by her own arm.

Unlike Lena's story, which we are given to understand probably has a happy ending, Eula's does not. When Hoake McCarron learns that Eula is pregnant, he refuses to take any responsibility and runs away to Texas. Eula's father arranges a marriage for her with his business partner, the insufferable Flem Snopes. Neither love nor honor means anything to Flem. His marriage with Eula is simply another commercial transaction. And so the matchless beauty of this little north Mississippi community is mated with a cold-blooded and almost inhuman man.

Having dealt with Lena and Eula, I want to say something about other of the characters who are, even if minor, almost invariably presented with vividness and intensity.

Some are women of strong and forceful character. Eula's mother is such a woman. She has borne seventeen children to Will Varner but this exploit has not depleted her energy or her cheerfulness. She is in fact a woman of coarse fiber. When told of Eula's pregnancy, she reproaches the bearer of this news for spoiling her nap.

Mrs. Beard, who runs the boardinghouse which figures in *Light in August,* shows compassion for Lena Grove when Lena arrives in town, pregnant and rather obviously, as most people rightly suspect, without any marriage certificate or wedding band. Faulkner seems to have had a soft place in his heart for these hardworking and rather down-at-the-heels women who eke out a living running small-town boardinghouses.

Mrs. Beard, by the way, exhibits a characteristic of many of the women in Faulkner's fiction. They are wiser than their menfolk; they almost instinctively make shrewd character judgments; they easily see through men's subterfuges. When the rather clumsy and certainly ingenuous Byron Bunch, the bachelor, brings Lena to Mrs. Beard's house, Mrs. Beard quickly sizes up the situation. She admires, but is half amused by, Byron's conduct. She quickly discerns that though Byron himself does not know it, he is already in love with this young woman whom he has barely met and whose story (namely, that she has come to rejoin her husband) is not very credible. But she immediately finds a room for Lena and takes her in.

Not all of Faulkner's women, however, are strong-minded. He presents many of them as victims—whether of their own weakness or because they knuckle under to unreasonable husbands, or are shackled by their fidelity to the marriage bond or simply by an overpowering love for their mates. Not even the most militant feminist could maintain that Faulkner has scanted this aspect of masculine truculence.

Mrs. Simon McEachern, in *Light in August,* is clearly browbeaten by her husband. McEachern is not a selfish or consciously cruel man. But he holds himself and his wife to a stern moral code. He is one of Faulkner's most straitlaced puritans. McEachern thinks of himself as a religious man, but the God that he worships is a God of strict justice. The McEacherns are childless, and they adopt out of the orphanage little Joe Christmas, but McEachern is the worst possible choice to be Joe's foster parent. What this child in particular needs is kindliness and genuine affection, and this is what it is not in McEachern to give. His wife is starved for affection and would smother the child in an almost mawkish motherly love if her husband would only let her. Even so, she manages to provide him on the quiet with special favors. But the boy is as stiff-necked as his foster father. He prefers the man's harsh justice to the woman's necessarily sneaking affection. As he puts it to himself, at least he knows where he stands with his foster father, but with his foster mother he does not. To Joe, women did not seem to play by strict rules, and so he had something like contempt for his foster mother and rejected all her attempts to mother him with her little secret indulgences. In distrusting her, he learns to distrust all women, and this, in his life as an adult, becomes Joe's tragedy.

As one would expect from any good novelist who writes of women, the love and sex relationship usually comes in for great emphasis. So it is with Faulkner. In *Light in August* a whole range of love relationships is exhibited. I have already mentioned Eula Varner, the preternaturally beautiful girl who is not at all interested in romantic love, who seems quite unconscious of her beauty and utterly indifferent to the sexual attraction that she exerts on almost every male. The young schoolmaster, Labove, who presides over the one-room schoolhouse at Frenchman's Bend, falls passionately, abjectly, obsessively in love with Eula when she is little more than a child, and burns with this love for her over a period of years. His emotion is a kind of madness, in which the man exalts the beloved woman to an almost supernatural status. Such love is often unhappy and even tragic, for it involves an emotional tension that mere flesh and blood can hardly sustain.

Labove's love for Eula—whose inner nature he hardly knows at all—is idealistic, but hardly spiritual. It flowers in Labove's imagination and is fed by all the pagan myths that he knows and all the love poetry he has ever read. Labove does not want to marry Eula. He simply wants to possess her physically one time. He felt, we are told, like a man with a gangrenous hand who longs for the blow of the ax that will sever it from his body forever.

One day when she is alone in the schoolroom he grasps her in his arms, but his attempted rape is abortive. We are told that Labove held the girl, "smiling [at her], whispering his jumble of fragmentary Greek and Latin verse and American Mississippi obscenity," when "suddenly she managed to free one of her arms," and once he was off-balance, "before he regained it, her other hand struck him a full-armed blow in the face. . . . 'Stop pawing me,' she said. 'You old headless horseman Ichabod Crane.'"

Later Labove waits for Eula's elder brother to come with a gun, for surely Eula will have told him what had happened. When he finds that she had simply brushed the whole incident aside as unimportant, Labove is stunned, humiliated, beaten. He immediately leaves Frenchman's Bend forever.

On the other hand, there is to be found in *The Hamlet* a pair of wholly dedicated and faithful lovers. They are Jack Houston and Lucy Pate. As children, Jack and Lucy go to school together, and Lucy comes early to regard Jack as the boy she means someday to marry. The boy resists. In fact, he is much annoyed at her shy overtures. Lucy is not aggressive. She is a properly brought-up girl. Some might even call her prim. But she is persistent. Her care and concern for Jack are revealed in a whole series of intimations which do not take the form of words but of small quiet acts, such as trying to do his homework for him. At last Jack, who has not the faintest desire to get married, to Lucy or anyone else, flees the country.

For seven years Jack lives with a woman whom he had met in and taken out of a Galveston brothel. But, responding to forces in him which he does not fully understand, he decides to go home. He divides such property as he has accumulated with the Galveston woman and, refusing her entreaties to stay, goes back to Frenchman's Bend, where he finds Lucy Pate still unmarried, apparently confident all along that Jack would someday return. They are married, and for six months they experience perfect happiness together.

Then Lucy, collecting eggs from the hens' nests, rashly goes into the stall in which Jack keeps his blooded stallion. Lucy is killed. Too late, Jack grabs his pistol and shoots the horse. Faulkner tells us that "he grieved for her for four years in black, savage, indomitable fidelity." When his death comes at the hand of Mink Snopes, who shoots him to avenge what he regards as an insult, we are ready to believe that for Houston death was almost welcome. No other woman can replace Lucy and he knows it.

In view of the popular notion that Faulkner never depicts normal, decent, human love, I am happy to present this instance of an inseparably bonded marriage. The story, of course, scarcely has a happy ending. But we don't go to a great artist to find happy endings. Life is not full of happy endings. Besides, happy love affairs do not always afford the best material for fictional treatment. We are grateful to have them in real life, but literary art thrives on conflict, difficulty, and unlikelihood. In short, in fiction we prefer to read how the great happiness was not attained effortlessly, but was striven for and finally won through difficulties and dangers. Even in real life a good marriage usually has to be earned.

The two novels that I have been discussing actually provide something like the whole gamut of types and kinds of love. They range from a kind of indifference to love, to the love of a simple woman responsive to her own instincts, to passionate even sacrificial love, to defeated and beaten love that has faded into not much more than a sense of duty mingled with an element of pity. We can add to this list the case of Bobbie Allen, the shabby little prostitute who introduces the young Joe Christmas to sex and with whom he has his first love affair. But Faulkner makes her much more than a mere stock character. Without for a moment sentimentalizing her, Faulkner reveals in Bobbie the last remnants of a sense of pity and tenderness.

I must add to this list one more name, that of Joanna Burden, one of the characters in *Light in August*. Earlier I did not include her in the major female characters along with Eula and Lena, but she is much more than a minor character. She certainly challenges comparison with the principal male character, Joe Christmas. Symbolically Joe and Lena represent the poles on which the novel turns: Joe is rootless, torn loose from nature, the masculine principle in an exacerbated and even violent form; whereas Lena is so closely allied to nature that she may seem a mere embodiment of it. She is the feminine principle almost in a state of purity. Yet in the plot action of *Light in August*, Joe and Lena never actually meet.

Yet if Lena and Joe represent polar extremes, so in some sense do Lena and Joanna. For in Joanna, the feminine principle has been badly distorted. I would place Joanna among Faulkner's several masculinized women. She has had little chance to be otherwise. She is the daughter of an arranged and, one supposes, a rather loveless marriage. She was brought up in relative isolation from the community, for the citizens of Jefferson regard the Burden family as carpetbaggers, Yankees who, after the Civil War was over, came into the town to stir up trouble. Joanna's father and brother had indeed been shot down by Colonel Sartoris at a polling place during the Reconstruction period. Although Joanna does not seem to be filled with bitterness at what had been done to her family, she certainly could hardly feel very friendly toward this hostile community. Her task, inherited from her family, has been to promote the advancement of the blacks, and this she seems to have done selflessly and well. But she seems to have had no very friendly social relations even with the black people whom she lived to serve. Nor had her grandfather, Calvin Burden, the abolitionist, loved the black man so much as he hated slaveholders. He had told Joanna as a child that God had put a curse upon the whole Negro race: it had been cursed to be forever "a part of the white race's doom and curse for its sins." He goes on to tell the child that the black race will be the "curse of every white child that was ever born. None can escape it." From that time forward, Joanna tells Joe, she came to see the Negroes "not as a people, but as a thing, a shadow in which I lived." The old abolitionist also tells Joanna that she must try to "raise the shadow with you. But you can never lift it to your level."

This is racist doctrine indeed. It finally poisons Joanna's attempts to serve the black race by making her motive for helping them, not a regard for them as fellow human beings, but an imposed duty, and one impossible to fulfill. Thus, in her own way, Joanna has been psychically as badly damaged as has Joe himself in his. To see just how badly Joe has been damaged, it may be necessary to make a brief résumé of what has befallen him.

Joe never knew his father or mother. He spent his earliest years in an orphanage and then his boyhood and youth with foster parents, the McEacherns. Mr. McEachern I have described as a stern Calvinist and his wife as a rather beaten-down, despairing creature.

Joe's youthful affair with Bobbie Allen and her betrayal of him completed his disillusionment with women and with sex. Joe's great aim is to secure his independence, to discover who he is, and his great virtue is that he never gave up his attempt to find out his own identity. But in his suspicion of the feminine principle, he also becomes hostile to nature itself. (Faulkner always associates women with nature: their instinctual life ran deeper and stronger than man's.) It would not go too far to say that Joe, in his straining away from the female world and his effort to raise himself above nature, was attempting to kick the very earth out from under his own feet. Such an effort is doomed to failure. It was, in effect, suicidal.

In Joanna's case, when this thoroughly repressed woman, lonely and needing love, whether or not she was conscious of the need, meets a man who is a kind of violent embodiment of the masculine principle, there is bound to be trouble. Indeed, it is no wonder that Joe eventually murders Joanna. Yet when they first come together, Joanna's very masculinity is attractive to Joe. When he approaches her door to ask for food, she is calm and matter of fact. She is living as a lone woman, in a house on the edge of town, but she gives no sign of being afraid. Later on, when Joe one evening attempts to possess her sexually, she resists, firmly but quietly. Her masculinization shows itself even here. Faulkner describes her struggle as the "hard, untearful and unselfpitying and almost manlike yielding of that final surrender."

For a while, Faulkner tells us, the pair "talked very little, and that casually, even after he was the lover of her spinster's bed. . . . It was as though there were two people, the person who by daylight talked about inconsequential things and the night-time person" with whom he lay in bed.

So the couple lived for a good while, she in the rundown old plantation house, he in a cabin on the grounds. In the dusk of one evening, they do begin to talk about matters of consequence. Here they share a kind of amity in which they open their hearts to each other. In this scene they might even seem to be a wedded couple, growing into some deeper understanding of each other. But this was not to last.

What Faulkner calls the second phase began. Joanna, once her repressions had been broken down, tries desperately to cram a whole lifetime's lovemaking into a few passionate months. The fury of her desires shocks even the world-hardened Joe. As Faulkner puts it, what shocked him was "the abject fury of the New England glacier"— Joanna was by blood and nurture a New Englander—"exposed suddenly to the fire of the New England biblical hell." The sense that she has committed a mortal sin seems to add intensity to Joanna's sexual pleasure. But with poor love-starved Joanna, what she craves is not merely sex as such. She rather pitiably wants romance too, the secret trysts and love notes that had been denied her in her girlhood.

Finally, this second phase comes to an end. Although Joanna has prayed, "Dear God, let me be damned a little longer, a little while," and again, "Not yet, dear God. Not yet, dear God," these fires of passion die out and the third phase begins in which she reverts to her old self. She starts to lecture Joe on the need to improve himself—to go to law school. She begs him to repent, to kneel beside her and pray for their forgiveness.

With this reversion to what Joe has learned to fear and hate in feminine behavior, he cuts her throat. It should be added, however, that just before he acts, Joanna draws out from the bedclothes an old Civil War ball-and-cap pistol and attempts to shoot Joe. But there is no explosion of powder—only the click of a misfire.

Years ago the literary critic Maxwell Geismar complained that Faulkner had made "this decent and well-meaning abolitionist spinster" the special object of his venom, that Faulkner had subjected her, as a Northern woman, to indignities that he would never think of visiting on a Southern woman. But this is to miss the point completely. Faulkner portrays Joanna with great compassion and dramatic sympathy. She is a long-suffering woman of resolution and fortitude. Faulkner respects her virtues and never denies her a proper dignity.

In any case, he has provided a brilliant psychological study of intense repression and what may happen to such a person. Joanna is thus the complete foil and counterpart to Lena, who remains close to nature and to her feminine instinctual life. In Faulkner's eyes, both women seem to have admirable virtues, though one comes to a tragic ending and the other, as the novel closes, seems on her way to a placidly happy future life.

I am tempted to use the story of Joanna Burden to make one more point, for it is an important one. Faulkner valued the feminine principle. He saw it as a principle of strength rather than of weakness. Human society needs it. Men in particular need it as a counterforce to their often reckless energies, which require being checked and channeled into fruitful enterprises. Nor is the feminine principle for Faulkner non-intellectual. He believed it was closely related to wisdom— wisdom of a life-sustaining kind. Joanna proves the case by negative example. She has courage, endurance, and resolution, but, through no fault of her own, she had to assume a man's duties and a man's role. If I read *Light in August* aright, Faulkner does not blame Joanna for her failure and her tragic ending. Who could have dealt properly with Joe Christmas, a man who had been turned, through his education and nurture, against the basic life principle? His inner sickness may well have been irreversible.

As I have argued elsewhere, this great novel is diminished if we regard it as merely a reflection of, and comment on, the Southern scene, or if we become obsessed with the issue of racial prejudice. Certainly, the novel is Southern, and certainly it presents a powerful indictment of bigotry. Yet its essential theme is much deeper and more universal. *Light in August* considers man and nature, the breakdown of the human community and consequent isolation of the individual, and, most of all, the fact and consequences of man's alienation. The tragedy of Joe Christmas is his alienation from womankind, from humanity in general, and from nature itself. In his descant on this theme, Faulkner joins the great international masters, T. S. Eliot and James Joyce, whose works he knew early and knew well.

Gavin Stevens
and the
Chivalric Tradition

Gavin Stevens makes his early appearances in Faulkner's work as a quite unimportant character. Through the late 1930s and the early 1940s, Faulkner used him in a number of detective stories, later to be incorporated in the volume entitled *Knight's Gambit,* or as a minor figure in stories like "The Tall Men" or "Tomorrow." Stevens does not become anything like a major character until we reach *Intruder in the Dust* (1949) and *Requiem for a Nun* (1951).

It can be argued, however, that in one story published before 1949, Stevens becomes something more than a detached observer. If not yet a really major character, at least he does more than comment and speculate on the actions of others. I refer to his role in the story entitled "Go Down, Moses," first published in 1941. Stevens dominates what little action there is. It is he who arranges to bring home the body of Samuel Worsham Beauchamp. It is the same kind of service that he had performed for Mrs. Hines when he saw to it that the body of Joe Christmas was sent back to Mottstown for burial. Stevens is a kindly man: he has a vein of disinterested concern for people in distress. Through him the community often finds a voice and sometimes a leader in some appropriate action, such as raising the funds to ensure

Given as a lecture at the 1975 Faulkner Conference at Oxford, Miss., and originally published in slightly different form in *University of Mississippi Studies in English,* XIII (1978).

that old Molly Beauchamp's grandson can come home and be buried "right."

In fact, Faulkner must have fairly soon discovered that he needed a character who could express the sometimes inarticulate feelings of the community and give it a voice. That is to say, Faulkner's very concern for a community made it highly convenient, if not actually necessary, for him to construct a character like Gavin. In an earlier essay in this volume, I argued that the very nature of a true community, especially a genuine folk community, ensures that its feelings are traditional and may even appear so unreflective as to seem spontaneous. The community does not have to call a special town meeting to find out how it feels and how it means to react to this or that event. There is all the more need, therefore, for the presence of a highly self-conscious person who can cogitate on events and try to interpret them to himself and to the reader. Note that I do not imply that Gavin always interprets them correctly. Frequently he does not. For example, Faulkner, in talking to the students at the University of Virginia, stated quite clearly that Gavin's explanation for Joe Christmas's peculiar conduct on the last day of his life was not necessarily the true explanation.

Yet as an interpreter Stevens does enjoy special advantages. He is literate. Although he has refused to break his ties with Jefferson, he has seen something of Europe and of Boston and New York. He is thus both outside the community and inside it. He has read deeply and widely. He likes to talk, but he is also willing to listen, and he evidently enjoys listening. We are told that though he "could discuss Einstein with college professors," he could also be seen "now and then squatting among the overalls on the porches of country stores."

Even before Faulkner created Gavin, he must have felt the need of a literate consciousness within the world of Yoknapatawpha. Thus we find such a character in the person of Horace Benbow in Faulkner's third novel, *Sartoris*. In what Faulkner had originally intended to be the published version, *Flags in the Dust*, though it achieved publication only in 1973, Horace attended Sewanee and later Oxford University as a Rhodes scholar. Give or take a little, Sewanee and Oxford are not a bad equivalent to Gavin's Harvard and Heidelberg. In *Flags in the Dust* we also learn that Horace had for a time toyed with the idea of becoming a priest in the Episcopal church. Fortunately, he eventually gave up the idea and went in for the law instead. I say "fortunately," for I think that the Reverend Mr. Mahon in *Soldiers' Pay* suggests the kind of parish priest Horace would have turned out to be: kindly, civilized, quite tepid, and rather more of a stoic than a Christian.

If this last conjecture amounts to futile speculation, it is nevertheless quite plain that Horace Benbow is made of softer metal than is Gavin. He is more of the aesthete, the dreamer, and in aspiration at least, he is a third-rate decadent poet. Moreover, he is half in love with his sister Narcissa, whereas the relation between Gavin and his twin sister Maggie is healthily normal.

I shall not, therefore, press for similarities between Gavin and Horace. Yet it is apparent that both men stick out above the surface of the Yoknapatawpha community like a pair of sore thumbs. Moreover, they are sufficiently alike for Faulkner to have made sure that the two never appear together in the same piece of fiction. *Sanctuary,* the last novel in which Horace Benbow does appear, was published in February, 1931, whereas "Smoke," the first story in which Stevens appears, was not published until April, 1931. As it turned out, then, Gavin Stevens succeeds Horace Benbow as Yoknapatawpha's resident intellectual. There is further evidence that Faulkner did associate the two men. In World War I, it is Horace who takes Montgomery Ward Snopes with him to an overseas post in the YMCA. That is the way it is reported in *Sartoris,* but in *The Town* it is Gavin Stevens who takes Montgomery Ward Snopes with him.

Our concern, however, is not with Horace Benbow but with Gavin Stevens, and so let us dismiss from further consideration Horace and, for that matter, other introspective and sensitive characters such as Quentin Compson, who, like Gavin and Horace, belongs to the company of Yoknapatawpha's introverts and idealists.

Gavin is not only an intellectual but a serious scholar. His pet project is to translate the Greek version of the Old Testament (that is, the Septuagint) into classical Greek—a project that has absolutely no scholarly value. It would amount to a philological *tour de force*. I assume that Faulkner was quite aware that he had set Gavin on a sort of dilettantish exercise and that he meant for his reader to recognize as much.

Gavin also has political concerns and has arrived at his own views on the Negro, the race question, the relation of the South to the rest of the country, and other matters.

On the matter of the black man and civil rights, Gavin is enlightened beyond most of his fellow citizens of Jefferson. He insists that the white Southerner grant forthwith the black Southerner his full civil rights, not only because such action is just, but because it is actually in the white Southerner's own self-interest. Yet Gavin's insistence that the Southern blacks could be truly freed only by the actions of the Southern whites puzzled, in 1949, and perhaps continues to puzzle today, readers of *Intruder in the Dust*. And in the same book, Gavin's description of the population of the coasts of the northeastern states as the "coastal spew of Europe" has won for neither Gavin nor Faulkner (who was assumed here to be using Gavin for his mouthpiece) any Brownie points from the liberals.

Gavin is a scholar and a born teacher as well. I have in mind his long talks with Chick Mallison in *Intruder in the Dust* and especially his tutelage of Linda Snopes in *The Town*. He feeds this schoolgirl not only ice-cream sodas but books and, in effect, his own lectures on art, music, and general culture. Gavin's sister Maggie refers to this business rather sardonically: Gavin is concerned with what he calls "forming her mind." But Maggie's tone of voice aside, she is dead right, and this is precisely what Gavin is doing. I mean to recur to this matter later on when we look at *The Mansion*.

Just now, however, I want to turn from Gavin as intellectual, as do-gooder, as scholar and thinker, to something that concerns not merely his intellectual but his passionate nature. What did he ask of love? What kind of woman did he love? What kind of woman did he marry? These are always important considerations for Faulkner, and they are important considerations for most of the rest of us. For to discuss a character merely in terms of his head, without saying anything about his heart, is to present a half man. Most of us are interested, whether in fiction or real life, in the whole man.

When we first meet Gavin, he is unmarried, and has the air of a confirmed bachelor. Gavin must have been born around 1890, and since he didn't marry until 1942, he remained a bachelor for some fifty years. But this is not to say that Gavin never fell in love. In fact, in *The Town* we learn that when he was in his early twenties he had fallen overwhelmingly and pathetically in love with Eula Varner. This would have been sometime after he had graduated from Harvard and before he left for Heidelberg in the spring of 1914.

By this time, of course, the beautiful Eula Varner had already been married for some years to Flem Snopes and, moreover, had already taken Manfred de Spain as her lover. Thus, Gavin's pursuit of Eula is from the outset hopeless. He clearly misjudges the situation. Against the confident, tough-minded, handsome, virile de Spain, Gavin has not a chance.

A single example will have to suffice: at the Cotillion Ball, Gavin is made furious at watching the way in which Manfred is dancing with Eula. Gavin steps up and jerks Manfred away from his partner. In a moment they are out in the alley to settle the difficulty and, as we expect, Gavin gets his face well bloodied for his pains.

A very shrewd assessment of Gavin's behavior is made by his nephew, Chick Mallison, who observes: "What he was doing was simply defending forever with his blood the principle that chastity and virtue in women shall be defended whether they exist or not." Gavin's picking a fight to defend Eula's chastity is surely quixotic. Eula had established a comfortable relation with de Spain. It is Gavin who is insisting that Eula's honor has been impugned, not the level-headed and matter-of-fact Eula. When there is a husband who feels no need to defend his wife's honor and a wife who doesn't insist that she has any honor worth defending, a stranger's insistence on defending it is folly compounded. Besides, Manfred and Eula were not caught *in flagrante delicto*. They were simply dancing somewhat shamelessly or, as Chick Mallison rather admiringly puts it, with "splendid unshame."

Gavin's sister Maggie is furious at what has happened and most of all at Eula's conduct. She thinks that Eula might at least have sent Gavin a flower. But Eula, according to her lights, is to do something more generous than that. Having come to realize Gavin's hopeless love for her, she goes up to his law office one evening and offers Gavin not a flower but herself—herself for at least the evening.

So we have the romantic young man of twenty-three, trembling with a desperate love for his Guinevere. Eula does not see herself as a Guinevere and, indeed, couldn't be more direct and explicit in her handling of the situation. Her first words of explanation for her visit are: "I thought it would be all right here. Better here." And when Gavin in shocked amazement repeats the word, "Here?" his goddess goes on to say: "Do it here. In your office. You can lock the door and I don't imagine there'll be anybody high enough up this late at night to see in the window. Or maybe—." And with this sudden new thought, she breaks off speaking and starts pulling down the shades.

Gavin is aghast. Unless he stops her, in a moment she will be pulling off her clothes. He does stop her—with a bitter taunt about her adultery with Manfred de Spain—and tries to show her the door. But Eula refuses to take umbrage, remains calm and practical, and in the course of the conversation that ensues, makes it plain that she has offered herself to Gavin not to persuade him to drop his lawsuit against her lover Manfred. She has come to Gavin simply because she knows that he is unhappy, and she goes on to say, "I don't like unhappy people. They're a nuisance."

This, from Eula, is the unkindest cut of all, and Gavin remarks bitterly, "So you came just from compassion, pity." Gavin is crushed, but he is also in a state bordering on terror. Twice, he blurts out, "Don't touch me." And when Eula orders him to "lock the door," Gavin says, "I might—would—have struck her with my out-flung arm, but there was no room."

In its shocking contrasts, in its sudden reversal of expectations, in its utter deflation of the passionate lover, the whole scene is comic; but it is much more than comic. It is blindingly revelatory of Gavin's character. What is his conception of love, after all? Note that Gavin is no high-minded young Joseph tearing himself out of the clutches of a Potiphar's wife, for he has known all along that Eula is a married woman. He is even sure—in his bones, at least—that Manfred de Spain is her accepted lover. Moreover, up to this moment on the very brink of consummation, he has claimed to be passionately in love with Eula. What kind of man is Gavin?

Note further that this confrontation with Eula is no temporary aberration. Gavin's attitude, as exhibited here, presumably has some relation to other aspects of his love life; for example, his failure to marry until he is fifty years old, and his failure to propose marriage to Eula's daughter Linda, though he had always manifested a great concern for her and though Eula had begged him to marry Linda.

Gavin's relation to women and his concept of romantic love, then, do call for some explanation. If these can be made comprehensible, perhaps we can throw light on his general idealism, his tendency to assume a posture of detachment, and his general preference for the contemplative life rather than active participation. Indeed, these aspects of his character have a bearing on his whole view of reality.

I do not, however, propose at this point to engage in a psychological analysis of Gavin. I doubt the efficacy of the method and, anyway, I lack the requisite expertise. What I plan to do instead is to relate Gavin's notion of love to the general tradition of the romantic passion as it has developed in the last millennium of Western civilization. In that millennium one can find it everywhere—in the troubadour poets of Provence, in the stories that developed in the Arthurian cycle of romances, such as the love of Lancelot for Guinevere or of Tristan for Iseult, in the nineteenth century as it shows itself in some of Wagner's music dramas, and in many great English and French novels, or (to come down to our own century) in the life and poetry of William Butler Yeats.

The best analysis of such romantic or chivalric love that I know of, however, is to be found in two books by Denis de Rougemont. They are, to give them their titles in English, *Love in the Western World* and *Love Declared: Essays on the Myths of Love*. Rougemont agrees with most of the other authorities in holding that chivalric love is a phenomenon of the last millennium in the West. You do not find it, for instance, in ancient Greece. It has apparently never existed in the Orient. Take note that Rougemont is not talking here about sex or about affection for a mistress or a wife, emotional patterns that are ubiquitous and universal. He is speaking of a special idealization of sexual love, a transcendent passion in which, for the man, the beloved woman becomes a kind of goddess. Romantic or chivalric love has—through its intense idealization—an affinity with the medieval cult of the Virgin Mary and, through its deprecation of all mere legalisms, an affinity with free love, the passion that scorns all the restraints imposed by society. Thus, Lancelot and Guinevere are chivalric lovers as Guinevere and her duly wedded and lawful husband, King Arthur, could not be.

In short, the courtly or chivalric lover wants something far more ethereal and transcendent than any mere union of the flesh, for his erotic longing is finally lodged in his head and not in his loins. Gavin Stevens, then, proves himself to be the true chivalric lover in refusing such a fleshly consummation when Eula offers herself to him, for

Gavin is in love with a dream, a dream, to be sure, that Eula seems to incarnate, but a dream nevertheless, and he refuses to relinquish that dream. It has far greater value to him even if the impossibility of realizing it renders him desperately unhappy. Eula's practical wish to ease his pain and make him happy misses the point completely.

Now, I do not mean that Gavin is necessarily fully conscious of all this. He need not be, and his emotional state on the evening that Eula entered his office was indeed obviously confused. But there need not be any confusion in our own minds about what is going on in this instance. Eula is, in Gavin's eyes, Guinevere or Iseult, the impossible she whom he must perforce worship from afar. But when she refuses to play Iseult to his would-be Tristan, when she refuses to be impossible—when she steps down from her pedestal and makes herself almost matter-of-factly available—we are not to be surprised that Gavin recoils in bitterness, anger, and even something like terrified revulsion.

Earlier I remarked that chivalric love refused what we would call a normal fulfillment in marriage. Rougemont argues that the troubadour poets were influenced by the heretical sect of Cathars. The Cathars, because of their ascetic distrust of the flesh, would have nothing to do with it; but less puritanical chivalric lovers, those who did not abjure sex as such, also had their case against marriage. For marriage, in the Middle Ages, among the ruling classes in particular, was often a marriage of convenience—a means for allying one family to another, for transferring lands and wealth, for securing coveted possessions. Certainly among the nobility, marriages were usually arranged, and if love developed, well, that was a pleasant dividend, but not essential. But, for the chivalric sensibility, true love was soiled by considerations of social and economic advantage. True love must be spontaneous and free.

Marriage, even to this day, has not stood very high in the tradition of romantic love. One of the section headings in Rougemont's *Love in the Western World* is "Marrying Iseult?." Marriage with Iseult is inconceivable, for to marry her is to have her "dwindle into a wife," as Congreve's Millamant phrased it. Or, as Rougemont puts it: "In countless nauseating novels there is now depicted the kind of husband who fears the flatness and the same old jog-trot of married life in which his wife loses her 'allure' because no obstructions come between them."

This tradition comes right on down into our own time. Hemingway, for example, cannot conceive of married love's being able to maintain the brilliant flame of romantic love. It is no accident, therefore, that he sees to it that his true lovers are incapable of union (as in *The Sun Also Rises,* since the hero has been emasculated by a war wound), or else that he has the heroine die in giving birth to her first child (as in *A Farewell to Arms*), or that events of the war limit the lovers to a mere three days of bliss (as in *For Whom the Bell Tolls*).

One finds a similar situation in Fitzgerald's *The Great Gatsby.* Gatsby is the true chivalric lover who lives in a dream and in a sense dies for a dream, whereas his beloved, Daisy, and her wealthy husband are not romantic lovers at all. They have a convenient arrangement together and they are eminently practical. Nick Carraway reserves his bitterest comment for them. He says: "They smashed up things and creatures and then retreated back into their money or their vast carelessness or whatever it was that kept them together." We may be sure that it was not a romantic love that kept them together.

To return to Rougemont for a moment: he remarks that there is one requirement absolutely necessary for chivalric love. It must not risk losing its intensity. Fulfillment threatens to diminish it. Continual fulfillment is almost certain to tame and domesticate it. Hence the need for some barrier that will make consummation difficult if not impossible. For the heretical Cathars of twelfth-century Provence, the very flesh itself, as we have seen, was a barrier to the almost morbidly "spiritual" love to which they aspired. The two souls strove to unite in one clean transcendent flame, and the very materiality of the bodies of the lovers got in the way. For the more fleshly troubadour poets, marriage itself proved a sufficient barrier: chivalric love was the all-but-hopeless adoration of the young landless knight, yearning for the lady of the castle whose husband was his liege lord. For Lancelot, it was his dangerous love for the king's wife, a love that had to be kept secret, yet to enjoy which he and Guinevere risked everything. The fact that such love was forbidden and dangerous gave it its special spice—as much of the art of Western civilization makes plain, from Wagner's *Tristan und Isolde* down to the fiction of our cheaper magazines and our class-B movies.

In sum, the real enemy of chivalric love, with its ardors and intensities, its fine-spun idealisms and quixotic denials and postponements of gratification, is permissiveness and ready availability. When the beloved woman becomes not a goddess, but simply a mammalian organism conveniently at hand, then the transcendental element necessary to chivalric love evaporates. Yet, as our own age is beginning to find out, humdrum conventional marriage is not the only enemy of rapturous love: the sex manual, the pornographic novel, and the X-rated movie could conceivably reduce love between the sexes to mere triviality.

In spite of the reputation of the rural South for violence and for earthiness, anyone who has known this region in Faulkner's day knows that it also tends to be straitlaced and prim on one social level, and fundamentalist and puritanical on another. Even today, it is probably the only section of the United States that still believes in the doctrine of Original Sin and, accordingly, perhaps the only section that takes sex really seriously—as a life-and-death proposition.

Rougemont's attempt to account for the development of chivalric love among the troubadour poets by adducing the influence of the puritanical and Manichaean Cathars has been criticized; and in his second book he plays down this earlier emphasis on such disparagement of the flesh. Nevertheless, the suggestion that chivalric love needs a certain kind of puritanism for its full burgeoning fits Faulkner's South like a glove. After all, who are Faulkner's great chivalric lovers? Labove, who belongs to a spartan family living up in the hills and who is something of an ascetic—he is described again and again as a kind of monk; Harry Wilbourne of *The Wild Palms,* who belongs to a hard-working, God-fearing Protestant background; Byron Bunch, who for years methodically rode to a little church miles out in the country to direct the singing; and Quentin Compson, who is, whether or not God-fearing, thoroughly squeamish and oversensitive on the whole issue of sex. In Quentin's case there is also the powerful barrier of incest—which he tries once to break through but cannot. Quentin is indeed one of Faulkner's chivalric lovers.

Another barrier that is still formidable even today is impuberty—as witness the stir raised in the 1950s by the publication of Nabokov's *Lolita.* Rougemont takes note of it in his *Love Declared* and actually borrows from *Lolita* the term *nymphet.* Is Linda Snopes for Gavin a kind of nymphet? Is Gavin doubly a chivalric lover in virtue of his curious ice-cream-parlor courtship of the daughter of Eula Snopes?

Well, yes and no. Gavin clearly never thinks of surmounting the barrier. He is careful to take no liberties with the young girl. Moreover, he is by nature generous and helpful. His feelings toward Linda are kindly, and they may be merely avuncular. I have no desire to try to make him out a dirty old man. But his relationship with Linda is obviously a very peculiar one—and later even more so when Linda has become a grown woman.

When Linda returns to Jefferson as a young widow, Gavin still does not propose to her, even though she tells him, "I just must be where you are," and later, more passionately, "Gavin, Gavin. I love you. I love you." What are his barriers? Men have in the past achieved happy marriages with women more than eighteen years younger than they. Eula begs Gavin to marry Linda. A number of Gavin's friends believe for a time that he will.

But Gavin does not marry her because, as I would judge, he does not dare to tamper with a romantic dream. Maggie, Gavin's very perceptive and practical sister, observes that one does not "marry Yseult." Linda is for Gavin at least Iseult's daughter—and he has already long before predicted for her the life of an Iseult: she will love once romantically and intensely, he insists, but will lose her love and mourn him forever after, unwilling to accept any second-best. Gavin has in this instance made one of those self-fulfilling prophecies. In love with the romantic dream himself, he has no intention—by marrying Linda himself—of preventing the prophecy's coming true.

Maggie has made her own prophecy: namely, that her brother will eventually marry a widow with four children. She misses absolute accuracy by only two children. Not bad, I should say; for in 1942, Gavin does marry Melisandre Backus Harriss, whom he had known as a girl. In short, it seems that Gavin felt in his bones that romantic love, in the grand passionate manner, should not mix with married love. Anyway, he doesn't risk it, and his perhaps unconscious sense that they are, or ought to be, incompatible is the best proof of the power that the myth of romantic love exerts on him.

Did Faulkner get these insights into the nature of chivalric love from reading Rougemont? No, he couldn't have, and he didn't need to. For Rougemont is simply summarizing and systematizing—though how brilliantly—what has been endemic in the culture of the West for a thousand years. Faulkner could have got what he needed to know from Gautier's *Mademoiselle de Maupin,* which we know he read, or from the early poetry of his favorite poet, W. B. Yeats, or from Tennyson's *Idylls of the King,* or from Wagner's operas, from the love songs of Tin Pan Alley, or even from the movies shown at Tyler's Air Dome picture show in Oxford, Mississippi.

Gavin Stevens aside, how important to Faulkner was the concept of chivalric love? Quite important, I should say. Look at *Soldiers' Pay,* or *Light in August,* or *The Hamlet,* or *The Wild Palms*—where the story of Harry Wilbourne and Charlotte Rittenmeyer deals almost exclusively with this theme.

What was Faulkner's attitude toward chivalric love? Did he take it seriously? Did he believe in it himself? These are good questions, too good to be answered with a confident *yes* or *no.* If we are trying to be accurate, we can say that Faulkner recognized chivalric love as a pervasive and important feature of our culture. It has given rise to some very great poetry, including Dante's *Vita Nuova.* And it has been the principal subject matter of the novel from its beginnings. Chivalric love has its tragic aspect, and in a novel like *The Wild Palms,* to take a notable example, Faulkner has allowed his lovers their tragic dignity. If chivalric love can be regarded as a kind of sublime folly—a passion so transcendent that for its sake the world is well lost, since no price is too great to purchase it—it can also be seen as foolishness unmitigated. Faulkner is thoroughly aware of the comic aspects of chivalric love. At times he is willing to laugh at the chivalric lovers, as he does when Eula's night visit to Gavin's law office knocks the stuffing out of that astonished young man. Even in *The Wild Palms,* Faulkner has not avoided certain comic implications. In the mining community in Utah to which Harry and Charlotte have retreated to avoid the infections of respectability and bourgeois society, they are driven by the intense cold to share the same bed with the lusty and uncomplicated Buckners. This pair shamelessly satisfy their sexual urges, but Harry and Charlotte, the romantic lovers that they are, are too fine-grained, too fastidious to do so. But they have fled to the wilderness to keep their love pure and unspotted from the world, only to find that they have taken the world into bed with them.

Yet, whether considered to be a sublime transcendence, or a foolish denial, of the flesh, the lover's tendency to etherealize his experience is one of the important elements in Faulkner's work. Consider the variety of chivalric lovers presented to us. I've already mentioned the young schoolmaster of Frenchman's Bend, Labove. Although one could hardly exaggerate the differences in background and personality between him and Gavin Stevens, Eula casts much the same spell upon them both; or perhaps we put it more accurately if we say that both men project upon Eula the same aura of divinity. For Labove, she is not the Iseult of Arthurian romance, but some divinity out of the Greek pantheon. But a divinity she is, and Labove is obsessed. Moreover, much more is involved than powerful sexual feelings. They are sexual and they are powerful, but they cannot be eased simply by visiting a brothel. They are driven up into Labove's head: they have become an obsessional erotic dream.

I could go on with other examples: Byron Bunch, the gallant little unhorsed knight who selflessly comes to Lena Grove's rescue, is at once comic and admirable and, in his own way, as mad—or irrational—as is Labove himself. I could even add Ike Snopes, the idiot, who is in love with Houston's cow. Even here, however, more than mere sex is involved. Ike rescues her from the grass fire; he garlands her head with a coronet of wild flowers. For Ike, the cow becomes a kind of goddess, like ox-eyed Juno, the wife of Jupiter, the queen of the classical pantheon.

Faulkner summons his greatest prose poetry to the task of making the reader see the cow as she appears in the idiot's adoring eyes. And here Faulkner needs his greatest prose poetry to enable us to grasp the fact that Ike too is a chivalric lover. For between this lover and his beloved, there yawns the most formidable barrier of all—more forbidding even than incest—bestiality, man and animal in sexual congress.

It is high time, however, to return to Gavin Stevens. In considering him as a lover, I have neglected other important aspects of his character and personality. But, of course, there is only so much that can be covered here. Yet, Gavin's concept of love does have a relation to the larger and more general issues and it will not hurt to make one or two brief suggestions about them.

First, Gavin's idealism (of which chivalric love is an aspect) is deep. Gavin is somewhat given to theorizing—as in his account of what Joe Christmas's white blood and black blood compelled him to do.

Second, there is the matter of Gavin's view of women and of reality in general. I believe that Faulkner would not have frowned on my linking so closely women and reality: he would agree that the idealist's ability to understand women—who constituted, in Faulkner's opinion, the basic, the essential, the practical half of humanity—is a reasonably good index of an idealist's grasp of reality itself. Maggie loves her brother Gavin and is aware of his solid virtues, but she worries about the way in which he fails to see what women are like, and she finds him unable to understand humanity in general.

Our last view of Gavin—it occurs at the end of *The Mansion*—is of a flabbergasted man. He had badly miscalculated Mink's undeviating determination to call Flem Snopes to account for repudiating clan loyalty. Gavin had really believed it was safe to get Mink pardoned and that for a bribe of five hundred dollars he would agree to leave the state of Mississippi. Worse still, Gavin had completely misunderstood Linda. He is utterly shocked to find that Linda, the woman who he feels must be protected from even the knowledge that Mink has refused the bribe and that her stepfather is in danger, has in reality connived all along to get Mink out of prison just so that he would have a chance to shoot Flem.

Gavin, who had so carefully formed Linda's mind and had got her to that romantic place, Greenwich Village, in order to fulfill his own romantic dream of what she should be and do, is very close to collapse at the end. We are told that Ratliff is as "gentle and tender as a woman" in opening the door of the car in which he will drive Gavin home. He asks Gavin: "You all right now?" and though Gavin exclaims, "Yes I tell you, goddammit," Ratliff is still solicitous of him, though in proper Ratliff style, he turns his concern into a piece of badinage. He remarks that he hopes that Linda has no daughter "stashed out somewhere," and that if she has, he hopes Linda will never bring her to Jefferson, for, as Ratliff puts it, "you done already been through two Eula Varners and I don't think you can stand another one."

Gavin, the idealist and do-gooder, the man who would like to believe the best of everybody, here ends up as a somewhat discomfited Don Quixote. (If you fancy the analogy, you can regard Ratliff as his realistic, no-nonsense squire, Sancho Panza.) Actually the general analogy is not too far-fetched. In fact, I shall claim that it fits my topic precisely. For surely Cervantes' Don Quixote de La Mancha is one of the great chivalric lovers of all time. His wonderful imagination turned a plain country girl (not nearly so beautiful as that staggeringly beautiful country girl Eula Varner) into the noble Dulcinea del Toboso, for the love of whom he embarked on all sorts of knightly adventures. Don Quixote is lovable and gallant, a true gentleman, but, like Gavin Stevens, somewhat impractical and not noted for realistic discernment. But what more pleasant compliment could Faulkner have paid to Gavin than to give him a slight resemblance to the courtly Don, the hero of one of his favorite novels, one which he tells us he read regularly once a year.

The
British Reception
of Faulkner

The story of Faulkner's rise to eminence in letters is too well known to require elaboration. His first novel, *Soldiers' Pay*, in 1926, received on the whole very favorable reviews, both in this country and in Great Britain, but after that, the response became indifferent or hostile. Most of Faulkner's fellow Southerners either did not read him or, if they did, resented what they felt was an effort to give the South a bad name as decadent and degenerate. The literary establishment, with headquarters in New York, was not concerned, of course, with whether or not the South's reputation was further blackened. The name of the South was already sufficiently dark in its books. In 1931, *Sanctuary* became something of a popular success, but as a scandalous book rather than one that the literary critic could take seriously. The result was that though Faulkner had by 1947 published all of his masterpieces and the great body of his work, only three of his novels were in print: *The Sound and the Fury* and *As I Lay Dying*, within the single covers of a Modern Library edition, and in another, *Sanctuary*, in lonely splendor or squalor.

This same condition was to be found throughout the English-speaking world, and though there were discerning readers on both

Given as a paper at the 1973 Symposium on Comparative Literature in Lubbock, Texas, and originally published in slightly different form as "The British Reception of Faulkner's Work," in *William Faulkner: Prevailing Verities and World Literature* (Lubbock, 1973).

sides of the Atlantic, Faulkner was not acclaimed as a great literary artist, and by most of the reading public, indeed, his work was scarcely
regarded as literary at all.

Only France as a nation comes out of this situation with any real
credit. The story of Faulkner's French reception has been told several
times. Suffice it for me to say that—for whatever reasons—the French
literary critics as a group rather quickly sensed what Faulkner was trying to do and asserted the success of his accomplishment. I have my
own notions as to why the French were more sensitive and more intelligent in this matter than were Faulkner's fellow countrymen or our
British cousins. But I mention the French here only by way of contrast, for my concern is with the fact of British misunderstanding, lack
of interest, and misjudgment.

My last sentence may seem a scandalously sweeping generalization,
and of course I am generalizing. In fact, in Britain as well as in the
United States, voices of understanding and appreciation were raised
early and steadily, from the beginning of Faulkner's publication to the
present day. I shall refer to some of them here, but I do not promise to
note them all. Rather, I shall simply indicate now, once and for all, that
I am aware of these minority reports. The general fact with which I
shall concern myself here is that the British reception of Faulkner is
still grudging, biased, and often amounts to indifferent dismissal. I believe that there are reasons to account for this, and in what follows I
shall examine some of these reasons.

It is only fair to the British, however, to say that in part their attitude toward Faulkner derives originally from the United States itself.
It is one of the ironies of the cultural situation that though the Old
South is closer to Great Britain in racial stock and in certain habits of
mind than perhaps most other parts of the United States are, the typical Britisher would be surprised to hear me say so. His picture of the
United States is pretty well controlled by what radiates from New York
and Boston. He tends to accept as correct the northeastern states' view
of the rest of the country. Thus, his notion of the South represents an
interpretation of someone else's interpretation. Since he comes by it at
second hand, the consequence is that he has—even less than the New
Yorker or the Bostonian—the impulse or the opportunity to clear up
his preconceptions by firsthand inspection.

I am quite deliberately emphasizing this matter of the British notion of the South, for it is an important factor in determining the British conception of Faulkner's art. If one examines typical British articles or book reviews on Faulkner, one notices how frequently occur such phrases as "Faulkner's depiction of the fellaheen Deep South," or Faulkner's appreciation of everything that "is relaxed, corrupt, and phosphorescent in the southern countryside," or Faulkner's depiction of human beings "who have been ruined in the slow stagnation of agriculture."[1]

Give a dog a bad name and it is easy to hang him. From the publication of *Uncle Tom's Cabin* on down to the latest editorial in the New York *Times,* the South has been depicted as a region of ignorance, cruelty, and racism. The South, of course, has itself to blame in great part for its bad repute. There have been ignorance, bigotry, and cruelty. But the bare facts do not fully account for the situation. The South has had its sins of omission and commission retailed to the world by a powerful and essentially hostile press—with all the magnification that such an arrangement entails.

In the past two decades, however, the whole of the United States has come to be seen as a culture wracked by violence, even unspeakable violence—bizarre murders and rapes and other modes of cruelty. Let me say that I am here less concerned with crime statistics—though they are grim enough—than with perceptions. The perception of the South as a special den of iniquity has somewhat gone out of fashion. There is enough depravity for everyone to have a share.

Yet the old perception may have lasted longer in Great Britain than in this country. When Joyce Carol Oates's first novel was reviewed in one of the more widely circulated London newspapers, the reviewer said that she "has been compared with Faulkner; and I see why. It isn't merely that her novel is set in much the same territory, the harsh, unfriendly sterile edges of the South. It is more that the characters are revealed as acting from their deepest and least civilized impulses." The clear implication is that the South is the appropriate region for such

---

1. I have gleaned these instances from Gordon Price-Stephens' valuable essay entitled "The British Reception of William Faulkner—1929–1962," *Mississippi Quarterly,* XVIII (Summer, 1965), 119–200. In the course of my own essay, except where I have specifically indicated the source of an article or review, the source may be found in the Price-Stephens study. Although I am so deeply indebted to Mr. Price-Stephens for my materials, I have, of course, given my own inflection to what I take to be their significance, and for that, Mr. Price-Stephens is obviously not to be held accountable.

uncivilized characters as Miss Oates portrays, though the reviewer did not face the issue that Miss Oates's account of American life was based on her earlier experiences in New York State and Michigan.

In its cover story on Miss Oates (for December 11, 1972), *Newsweek* had a good deal to say about her penchant for violence and about the energetic depravity of the world depicted in her fiction. But *Newsweek* simply accepted that world as part of our own time and perhaps as a reflection of Miss Oates's own imagination. *Newsweek* had no allegations to make about the depravity and degeneracy of the Detroit area.

I sum up this particular issue by saying that in British reviews and articles on Faulkner, as in their American counterparts, the stereotype of the South remains a disturbing presence; it often serves to vindicate the writer's various dissatisfactions with Faulkner. I find that it usually remains a malodorous red herring, surreptitiously or sometimes even ostentatiously dragged across the trail.

Closely related to Southern depravity, real or imagined, is what is taken to be Faulkner's special subject matter. Reviewers who like Faulkner defend him for exposing the brutality and violence of the region. Reviewers who dislike Faulkner charge him with exploiting sensational material for its shock value, with the implication that he is either indifferent to human values or actually delights in the fact of corruption. One British reviewer, for example, observes rather sadly: "To see literary talent thus spent upon a morbid theme is sad. No moral or aesthetic purpose is fulfilled when the action is carried out by characters devoid of any interest except to the neurologist and the criminologist." From another British critic, Faulkner receives a kind of backhanded compliment. Faulkner's description of the hideousness of the Memphis brothel to which Temple Drake is taken represents "a new contribution . . . to literature."

Yet something more is involved here than merely the British equivalent of the American genteel tradition. The reviewers and critics that I have been citing are not all of them nice Nellies. One of them is, in fact, that redoubtable and usually perceptive observer, Rebecca West. Yet few of the British observers have been able to discern what Faulkner is doing with subjects apparently so repulsive, and their inability to see it raises certain questions.

This inability is often the result of the haste and carelessness with which many British reviewers write. I remember being bowled over by an English friend telling me that sometimes he would be sent as many as seventy books in a month to review—not that he was supposed to write about them all. It was expected that he would skim through them, discard some, do no more than mention others, and concentrate on a few. But even after such generous discardings, how could one find time to read with any thoroughness those books serious enough to demand a careful reading? It is no wonder that one discovers the tell-tale signs of superficial reading in so many reviews of Faulkner.

Let me adduce some examples, most of which I have gleaned from Gordon Price-Stephens's essay. One British writer placed Faulkner's Oxford in the state of Missouri. An anonymous reviewer, writing about *The Hamlet* in the Glasgow *Herald,* consistently turned French-man's Bend into Fisherman's Bend. A writer in the London *Evening News* described *Sartoris* as a "study of a young Virginian returning from the great war." A contributor to the *Sphere,* Cecil Roberts by name, though stating that he had "read with care—and difficulty—every page of *Light in August,*" described the theme of the novel as *"the adolescence and revolt of a youth in a backwoods family in Alabama."* From the viewpoint of the British Isles, Mississippi is evidently inter-changeable with Missouri or Alabama or even Virginia. All these states are in some far-off outlandish region across the sea. Mr. Price-Stephens in a footnote sums up another whole cluster of such errors by observing that "many notices [contain] errors which indicated su-perficial readings. Addie Bundren was sometimes called Annie, or Ad-die Burden; Cash had his injured leg amputated, according to one ac-count, while another gave the broken leg to [his brother] Darl; finally, an anonymous writer in *The Glasgow Herald* . . . changed the Bun-drens' . . . team," which hauled Addie's coffin and her family to Jeffer-son, from a pair of mules to a pair of bullocks.

More serious consequences of careless reading have to do with char-acter and theme. Thus, Pamela Hansford Johnson describes the basic action in Faulkner's brilliant "The Fire and the Hearth" as one "con-cerning a cuckold making up his mind to kill his wife's lover." This story is one of the finest pieces in *Go Down, Moses.* Lucas Beauchamp as a young man had been sent for the doctor when Zack Edmonds's wife was brought to childbed and there were difficulties in her giving birth. Lucas somehow gets across the flooded river and comes back with the doctor, but not in time. The mother dies, but her child survives, and Lucas's wife Molly, who has herself only recently given birth to a child, takes up residence in the white man's house in order to take care of both babies. For six months Lucas endures this arrangement and then suddenly, feeling that his honor has been wounded, is overwhelmed with a compulsion to confront the white man and kill him. But he scorns to kill him without warning; each man—they had been childhood companions—strictly observes a code of honor. Each is careful to give the other "his chance." Lucas throws away his razor. The white man lays his pistol on the bed where, with equal chance, they can struggle for it. Lucas succeeds in getting it and fires point blank at Edmonds, but the shot is a misfire. Later, Lucas, all passion spent, his masculine identity asserted and honor satisfied, muses upon his good fortune: as he puts it, his white ancestor, old Carothers McCaslin (who is also the ancestor of his opponent, Zack Edmonds), came "and spoke for me." That is, Old Carothers respected his descendant's spiritual agony and intervened with the powers that be so that Lucas would not have to pay the price, which he had made up his mind to pay, for his vengeance, death at the hands of a lynching mob.

It is by no means certain, by the way, that Zack Edmonds was Molly's lover—in fact, it seems to me most unlikely that he ever was. In any case, Miss Johnson's summary is simply inadequate. As Price-Stephens puts it, "To describe the occasion so blandly, as though it were no more than an affair in middle-class suburbia, was to miss most of its significance."

Yet it was hardly carelessness in the usual sense that induced F. R. Leavis in 1933 to write that Joe Christmas remains essentially a "monotonously 'baleful' melodramatic villain whose mysteriousness is of so familiar a kind, depending upon your having only a surface to contemplate." Joe Christmas—and surely what I say here does not represent merely my own opinion—is one of the most dazzlingly brilliant of Faulkner's creations. Moreover, we are given much more than a surface to contemplate. The whole central section of the novel is devoted to an account of Joe's life from babyhood to manhood in order to show just how Joe's character was formed.

And simple carelessness will not account for the many misinterpretations to be found in Martin Green's *Re-appraisals: Some Commonsense*

Readings in American Literature.[2] His comments on the subject of Jason Compson's "sanity" stem not from "common sense," but from a lack of imagination and an insensitivity to literary effects. To make these harsh judgments stick, however, I need to examine a few in detail.

In the Appendix to *The Sound and the Fury* (a long biographical and genealogical note added by Faulkner years after the novel was published), Faulkner observes that Jason Compson was "the first sane Compson since before Culloden." Faulkner describes Jason as "logical rational contained and even a philosopher of the old stoic tradition." Mr. Green observes that it "needs no proof that Jason is not particularly sane; he is scarcely even rational," and he goes on to argue that the real point of Faulkner's remark "is to imply that Quentin, Caddy, and Mr. Compson are all *in*sane. . . . We gather that it is more 'normal,' it is 'better,' to behave like Jason than like the other three."[3] Yet any but the most obtuse reader will regard Faulkner's calling Jason "sane" as bitterly ironical. Of course, Jason is not particularly sane and is scarcely even rational. Jason Compson, to be sure, thinks of himself as completely rational. Throughout the third section of the book, which is a continuous monologue spoken by Jason, he parades his possession of an uncompromising rationality. He has no room for sentiment of any kind. Yet surely Faulkner's point is that Jason's sister Caddy, and his brothers, including Benjy the idiot, are far more fully human than he; and Faulkner clearly implies that unless there is in a man some outpouring of generous emotion, some concern for more than the brass tacks of life, a man is not human at all. Better to be *in*sane with Quentin and Caddy—even if their affections on occasion turn into passionate folly—than to be "sane" with Jason. (It is embarrassing to have to spell these matters out, but Mr. Green's stiff literalism demands it.)

It is easy to see where Mr. Green's literalism comes from. It is the result of his application to Faulkner of a doctrinaire formula. He has stated it for us in almost capsule form. He asks himself the question, What, then, does Faulkner believe in? He answers: "Only in the consciously ambiguous or the aggressively inadequate; which is a form of

---

2. Martin Green, *Re-appraisals: Some Commonsense Readings in American Literature* (London, 1963).

3. William Faulkner, *The Sound and the Fury* (New York, 1946), 16; Green, *Re-appraisals*, 189.

unbelief. This is what makes the Appendix to *The Sound and the Fury*, and so much else of Faulkner's, almost classically bad writing. This enormous rhetoric is inspired by something that denies itself, something that only half exists. . . . This mood of unbelief is the inspiration of the rhetoric. . . . [Faulkner] constructs an enormous universe to demonstrate the way things are *not*. The smell of death is over it all." [4] Thus saith Mr. Green. No wonder that, held in the grip of a generalization so sweeping as this, his boasted "commonsense readings" of Faulkner smack of a brittle and rigid "sanity" not unlike that of Jason Compson.

If I seem too harsh, then please consider one more example of Mr. Green's insistence that Faulkner speak by the card—that is, by the card devised by Mr. Green. He quotes a passage from *Light in August* in which two people at the planing mill are discussing Joe Brown, an obviously worthless person who has recently been hired for work at the mill. The passage that Green quotes reads:

> Mooney said: "Well, Simms is safe from hiring anything at all when he put that fellow on. He never even hired a whole pair of pants."
>
> "That's so," Byron said. "He puts me in mind of one of these cars running along the street with a radio in it. You can't make out what it is saying and the car ain't going anywhere in particular and when you look at it close you see that there ain't even anybody in it."
>
> "Yes," Mooney said. "He puts me in mind of a horse. Not a mean horse. Just a worthless horse. Looks fine in the pasture, but it's always down in the spring bottom when anybody comes to the gate with a bridle. Runs fast, all right, but it's always got a sore hoof when hitching-up time comes."
>
> "But I reckon maybe the mares like him," Byron said.
>
> "Sho," Mooney said. "I don't reckon he'd do even a mare any permanent harm."

Green's comment is that this is an exercise in "folk metaphor, not a conversation." But who is demanding that it be a conversation? Green himself, in order to establish his claim that Faulkner is always willing to sacrifice realism to a display of his rhetorical techniques. Here, he asserts that Faulkner "gives his characters, for example, dialect words, and country images even when he is making them do things in every

---

4. Green, *Re-appraisals*, 190.

profound sense at variance with their social and psychological types. When [Faulkner] has a point to make, or even just a metaphor to use, he rides roughshod over personal and social psychology." [5]

But there is no sacrifice of realism here. I have myself heard hundreds of such exchanges in the South—from whites and from blacks. Mooney and Bunch are vying with each other to see who can put the case against Brown more tellingly. Although this conversation may not seem very "realistic" to Mr. Green, it will seem thoroughly so to anyone who knows the folkways of the American South.

Martin Green is not, alas, the only reader who has been put off by Faulkner's rhetoric. In general, Faulkner's style has been a stumbling block for many British, as it has been for many American, readers. Let me cite a few British comments on his style as found in what is commonly regarded one of his very greatest novels, *Light in August*. One of Faulkner's more severe British critics writes that if a particular passage (which he quotes) had been "turned in by a school-boy in the English paper of his examination for the School Certificate, he would receive about fifteen per cent marks. No examiner would find it significant. He would find it merely incompetent."

That veteran man of letters Compton Mackenzie cited another passage from *Light in August* and commented: "Writing like that is the result of weakness masquerading as strength. Mr. William Faulkner has only to develop such a style a little further to collapse as utterly as so many other modern writers have collapsed . . . under the burden of words." And F. R. Leavis, though he admired aspects of this book, was also unhappy about its style. He found Faulkner's technique generally "an expression of—or disguise for—an uncertainty about what he is trying to do."

Typical British critics regard this alleged incompetence in style as leading to all sorts of other weaknesses. Because of his floridly rhetorical style and his poor handling of narrative techniques, Faulkner simply makes it too difficult for the reader. Mr. Price-Stephens provides us with a roll call of distinguished names who utter with greater or lesser vehemence this condemnation. They include those of Cyril Connolly, Edwin Muir, C. Day Lewis, Humbert Wolfe, Graham Greene, Philip Toynbee, and George Orwell.

5. William Faulkner, *Light in August* (New York, 1950), 32; Green, *Re-appraisals*, 177, 176.

Humbert Wolfe found *Absalom, Absalom!* "one of the most confused books ever written by a person of great talent." Graham Greene,
on the evidence of this novel, removed Faulkner at once from the company of Joyce and Gertrude Stein, and pushed him toward the British
equivalent of the Book-of-the-Month Club. There, Faulkner might
find fit audience though many. George Orwell, in writing of *The
Hamlet,* deposed that the whole book was written in what was, to put
it mildly, a fatiguing style. "The difficulty of reading it," he writes,
"comes from the fact that Mr. Faulkner crams into each sentence
thoughts which occur to him in passing but which have not necessarily much to do with the matter in hand." Orwell confessed that
"after a careful reading of *The Hamlet,* I must record that I have quite
failed to discover the plot of the story. All I can say with certainty is
that it is about some people somewhere in the Southern States of
America, people with supremely hideous names—names like Flem
Snopes and Eck Snopes—who sit about on the steps of village stores,
chewing tobacco, swindling one another in small business deals, and
from time to time committing a rape or a murder." There is, by the
way, one murder in *The Hamlet* and, unless my memory deceives me,
no rapes at all. Eula Varner is not raped, nor is Ettie Snopes. Can it be
that Orwell regards the idiot's sexual congress with the cow as an instance of rape? One would have expected Orwell to include it under a
rather more special rubric. At any rate, he somberly concludes: "A second reading—and to read a book of this length is several days' work—
might extract something more definite, but it is my honest opinion
that it would not be worth while."[6]

I shall not argue that Orwell's view is completely typical or that his
influence was so great that it was he who shaped Faulkner's British
reputation. But his last comment beautifully sums up what has been
true of very many British readers of Faulkner—quite generally and
from almost the beginning. Even the ordinarily sensitive and careful
reader found Faulkner almost impossibly difficult to read; worse still,
most such readers were easily convinced that there was nothing in
Faulkner of sufficient worth to justify any effort to read him.

Of the widely known British commentators on Faulkner, Cyril
Connolly seems to be by far the most complacent. Moreover, his own

---

6. Wolfe in *London Mercury,* XXXV (March, 1937), 517–18; Orwell in *Time and Tide,*
November 9, 1940, p. 1097.

prose, at least in the review I shall be citing, is also the most loose and ungirdled. The novel with which Connolly had to concern himself here is, I grant, far from one of Faulkner's best. It is *Pylon*. But if the novel brings to a reader's attention some of Faulkner's least able work, it brings out the very worst in Connolly himself. Thus Connolly writes: "The morbidity of [Faulkner's imagination] is beyond suspicion; he excels above all in combining a passionate hatred of the city, every sputum of which is familiar to him, with an appreciation of everything that is relaxed, corrupt, and phosphorescent in the southern countryside."[7] Since Faulkner was a country boy, he may well have had a countryman's normal suspicion of the city. But the city in *Pylon* is obviously New Orleans, a city in which Faulkner lived rather happily for a good many months, in which he wrote his first novel, and for which he seems to have entertained a good deal of affection. Connolly has mistaken for Faulkner's personal hatred for cities as such, the city portrayed as the impersonal background—strange, indifferent, and perhaps hostile—against which the homeless and almost penniless vagabonds of the air play out the drama in which their fortunes and even their lives are at stake. The holiday crowds that come to see a spectacle will always seem indifferent to the fate of the gladiators. I see nothing especially anti-urban in this.

As for Faulkner's love for the countryside: what attracts Faulkner to it is certainly not its corrupt and phosphorescent aspects. (The metaphor concealed in Connolly's prose is that of fox fire—a decaying bit of organic material, flowering in a swamp.) What Faulkner really loved in the Southern countryside is clearly revealed in the great hymns to nature to be found in *The Hamlet* or in *Go Down, Moses*. It is not the corrupt and decaying but the unwearied immortality of nature, changeless in spite of all its changes.

But I interrupt Mr. Connolly; he goes on to say: "It was this mingling of the vice of the town with the decay of the country, Popeye's city's [*sic*] clothes reflected in the tropical bogwater, that gave *Sanctuary* its extraordinary quality."[8] But the water that reflected Popeye's city clothes was the water of a clear running spring, where one might happily drink. And the point that Faulkner was making there was Popeye's contempt for nature, a contempt expressed by his spitting

---

7. Connolly in *New Statesman and Nation*, April 13, 1935, p. 525.
8. *Ibid.*

into the spring, and his fear of nature as expressed in his blind terror when an owl swoops near him.

What really disturbs Connolly, however, is what disturbs so many of his fellow countrymen: the difficulties of Faulkner's style. He remarks of one of the chapters of *Pylon* that its style "with its rolling turgidity, forced images, and cumbrous and uncouth eye to the main chance— the scarifying of the reader—is often pure Dreissler."[9] Connolly's own style is here so remarkable that I can't forbear commenting on it. In the first place, the writer to whom he refers is obviously Theodore Dreiser, though it may have been the typesetter who altered his name and not Mr. Connolly. In the second place, why does Connolly tax Faulkner with having used forced images in view of the forced images that he himself uses? Can a style—Faulkner's or even Mr. Connolly's— be said to have a "cumbrous and uncouth eye"? What, for that matter, is an uncouth eye? Not to mention a cumbrous eye.

In concluding his review, Connolly observes that "the great advantage of the English writer over the American is superior education— what are the masterpieces that the Americans can't copy? *Ulysses, The Waves, The Flower Beneath the Foot, South Wind,* works of imaginative scholarship. How far behind follow Glenway Westcott, Thornton Wilder and Carl Van Vechten!"[10]

Evidently Faulkner trudges some furlongs behind even these gentlemen. But I am concerned here with the revelation of tell-tale bias toward a certain kind of novel and a certain kind of prose more than with Mr. Connolly's complacency. How could one expect him and men like him to take easily or readily to the sort of fiction that Faulkner serves up? There is a kind of well-bred quality in the works that he is citing— even in *Ulysses,* if we are willing to let it count as an English novel— that makes them look cozy beside Faulkner's typical fiction.

Notable in this record of failures is the quality of the readers who failed. As Chaucer put it long ago, if gold will rust, then what will iron do? The failure has not been complete, of course, and it is a credit to the sensitivity of certain British literary figures who, in spite of the acknowledged difficulties, have discerned power and vitality in what seemed to many an uncouth fiction. V. S. Pritchett, for example, though he admitted the difficulty of Faulkner's style, especially for

9. *Ibid.*
10. *Ibid.,* 526.

an English reader who lacked "the necessary links with the Southern Negro and poor white cultures," nevertheless argued that Faulkner's method was valid and, further, that "the true justification of the method [employed by Faulkner] is that it creates the South in depth as, I think, no other part of America has been created by a novelist since the time of *Huckleberry Finn*."

David Garnett surmounted in even more decisive fashion the problems set for a British reader by Faulkner's style. In a very acute article published in the *New Statesman and Nation,* he wrote with reference to Faulkner's story "Red Leaves" that at a first reading, "the early pages seem to out-parody any parody. It [was] almost insulting that an artist should [have thought he could] produce his effects by means of such boorishness." But, on a second reading, Garnett testifies, the reader's initial sense of sloppiness and dreadful incompetence finally gives way to delightful astonishment. Garnett writes:

> It [was] with some such astonishment that I [reread] *Red Leaves* which unfolds itself slowly, almost unintelligibly: before one's eyes the worm sloughs its skin, spreads its wings to dry and flickers away in glory. It is a magnificent, a marvelous story, a work which only a great creative artist could have written. Caliban, taking us by the hand and introducing us to Prospero's island could not produce more of a surprise, for Faulkner takes us into an unimagined world, absolutely fantastic and absolutely convincing. Read it again and where is the boorishness, where are the insults to the reader, where the comic clumsiness bound to defeat the parodist? Oddly enough these qualities have entirely vanished.[11]

Garnett's judgment of the quality of the story is dead right and, for its time, almost unique. In fact, I think that even today, "Red Leaves" is scarcely given its due by people who think of themselves as Faulkner enthusiasts. Even more interesting is the fact that Garnett was able to see on his second attempt that the apparent unintelligibility, needless difficulty, and crudity were in fact part of the art and, once seen in proper perspective, were revealed as brilliant devices for presenting the story.

Perhaps I am inclined by temperament and training to dwell too long on this particular point, but I think it an important one. Can

11. Garnett in *New Statesman and Nation,* September 30, 1933, p. 387.

there be real badness of style if vitality and power inhere in the work that employs such a style? In fact, isn't the excellence of any style measured by the very intelligibility and power of the story or the poem or the drama in question? Can one say that the author's world view or his vitality or his energy or the importance of his subject matter really makes up for a trivial or clumsy or impoverished style? For if he does say so, then obviously he implies that the style is a merely superficial decoration to the content; indeed, he commits himself to a real separation of form and content—as if in works of art a true separation between them were possible. For how can we know the content except through the form?

This is not an extreme position that I am taking here. I freely concede that minor incidental blemishes occur even in great writers such as Milton and Shakespeare; and Faulkner, as a self-trained, self-educated artist, surely had his. Occasionally it appears that he did not know the standard meaning of a word. Rather often—particularly in his novels of the late 1940s and 1950s—he involved himself in an obtrusive rhetoric. From first to last, there are minor blurs and obscurities in his work. But truly serious faults in form and style do a serious injury to the work itself—that is why we call them *serious* faults. Conversely, if the work impresses the reader with its truth and power, he would do well to reassess his previous strictures on its style and form. Perhaps they have served the purpose better than the first reading had indicated. Indeed, what looks to the reader at first as faultiness may prove to possess positive virtue. A good many British articles and reviews show confusion on this matter. Thus, the critic will slam the daylights out of Faulkner for alleged faults of style, and then proceed to pay him a left-handed compliment by saying that even so, the work possesses a strange power. Yet few of those who damn the form but praise the power of the achievement take the trouble, like Garnett, to reread in order to see whether the reprehended style may not after all be effective.

To illustrate: Howard Spring writes, "Hampering himself with every disability, Mr. Faulkner nevertheless achieves a triumph such as few novelists can reach." This is a generous tribute, but should not Spring have made his sentence read: "Though *apparently* hampering himself with every disability . . ."? In another instance, an anonymous reviewer of *Absalom, Absalom!* concludes: "The book has almost everything against it—a tiring prose, an exasperating method, a distasteful subject matter dubiously attaining the dignity of the tragedy it hints at. Yet the author's very passion, that conflicting love and hate finding no rest or resting-place, gives to its pages indubitable vitality; it lives as unquestionably, and if too often as awkwardly then sometimes also as beautifully, as others of Nature's more eccentric creations."[12] Again, the compliment to Faulkner is handsome and just. But it represents a triumph of the reviewer's sensibility over his own grotesque literary theory. How does he imagine Faulkner conveys his "indubitable vitality" if not through his prose and his narrative method? Does he do it with mirrors? Is the author's restless passion a kind of bodiless ectoplasm that hovers wraithlike over the pages of his novel? Let us remember that it is prose, whether tiring or exhilarating, that is the flesh and blood of any novel. No author can bring his mind into direct contact with the reader's without the mediation of words. If the words are truly a nonconductor, then no current of passion can flow from mind to mind. No author can dispense with the medium and no serious literary critic should dispose of it in so cavalier a fashion. As for the unpleasantness of the subject matter: what is the relevance of raw subject matter? Is the raw subject matter of *Macbeth* or *King Lear* really very pleasant? Isn't the real point here that Faulkner's imagination has redeemed into meaning what would have otherwise been dismissed as unpleasant? A critical theory that allows one to conceive of a work of art as a kind of pudding out of which one can pull few or many indubitable plums is not good enough to produce good practical criticism.

Thus, if I had to name a specifically national defect to account for the generally melancholy record of British estimates of Faulkner, I would cite poor critical theory: I mean good old British literary amateurism, which at its best yields a deft, light-fingered, graceful literary commentary, but which at its worst produces a peevish, wrong-headed, often ill-informed account that is designed to show off the reviewer's spiteful wit rather than to acquaint the reader with the character and quality of the work under judgment. In its own way, such amateurism is quite as bad as its polar opposite, American literary professionalism, which, when *it* fails, solemnly parades the obvious or indulges in irre-

12. *Times Literary Supplement*, February 20, 1937, p. 128.

sponsible symbol-mongering, or hunts down archetypal boojums—all in clanking PMLA prose. The long-suffering Faulknerian is moved to utter a heartfelt "Plague o' both your houses."

Since this essay was first published in 1973, its appraisal of the British reaction to Faulkner can scarcely pretend to be up to date. Moreover, I must confess that I have not undertaken a systematic canvass of the present state of affairs in Great Britain. My impression, however, is that the situation has not markedly changed. The reviews of books by Faulkner and about Faulkner in the *TLS* reflect a kind of cautious respect rather than genuine approval. Yet there are and always have been exceptions. In 1985, for example, I heard an excellent paper on Faulkner delivered by a young British scholar at the international Faulkner conference in Japan.

Faulkner and Christianity

The obvious way to find out what Faulkner thought of God and Christianity would be simply to ask him. Or, since we cannot now put such questions to him directly, to read what he told the students at the University of Virginia when they put these questions to him and to read also what he told interviewers when they asked him about his religious beliefs. So one gets out *Faulkner in the University* for the question-and-answer sessions at Virginia, or *Lion in the Garden*, a volume in which all Faulkner's interviews are collected. But many of his statements are vague or puzzling, or even contradict what is said in other passages. I think we do best therefore to look at his fiction—that is, to study the way in which his characters behave and to note his implied judgments, as author, of their actions and beliefs. After all, like that of most modern Americans, Faulkner's theological education was shaky. But he was a very great literary artist, and we discover the most profound and heartfelt of his beliefs when they are expressed in his art.

This is precisely what John Hunt has done in *William Faulkner: Art in Theological Tension* (1965). I find in it little or no reference to *Faulkner in the University*. As for *Lion in the Garden*, that book was not available to Hunt when he was making his own study.

The tension that Hunt finds in Faulkner's art is a tension between stoicism and Christianity. Yet Hunt goes on to say that both a general

Given as a lecture in 1985 at Wheaton College, Wheaton, Ill.

and a detailed look "at Faulkner's world would support the conclusion that his religious center is essentially Christian humanism and that the humanistic side of his Christian religiousness arises from his Stoicism. The Stoic tradition is judged from the point of view of a Christian religiousness which admits its truth but does not admit its unqualified adequacy and relevance." Hunt finally sums up as follows: "Faulkner's religion is a Christian Stoicism, or better, a Stoic Christianity, since endurance and pride and courage and compassion and sacrifice ultimately have a Christian relevance in Faulkner's fiction."

Some may feel that I am serving up quite a mouthful to swallow at one gulp. Some may also think that it is more than a little odd for me to state Hunt's conclusion, or any conclusion at all, at the beginning. But there is method in my apparent awkwardness. As I shall adduce examples from Faulkner's novels, you will have an opportunity to chew over and, I hope, even digest this rather formidable theological mouthful. There is an additional advantage in laying down at the very beginning a thesis which can then be illustrated, commented upon, and qualified as we consider what Faulkner's characters are actually made to do and say.

We might begin with Faulkner's very first novel, *Soldiers' Pay*. It will provide a forecast of Faulkner's general view of our situation as shown in his subsequent novels. In *Soldiers' Pay*, he presents a period of disillusionment and even despair, with the Christian beliefs under heavy stress, but the Christian virtues are still evident, though appearing in very unlikely places. Institutionalized Christianity proves to be ineffective and even irrelevant. It does survive, however, in the primitive communities. There also survives in this Southern community a kind of innocent pre-Christian paganism, spontaneous, instinctive, close to nature. Both it and the Christianity held by those of simple faith seem to Faulkner more admirable than so much of conventional Christianity.

When Faulkner visited Japan, an interviewer asked him point blank whether at this present time he believed in Christianity. Faulkner gave this answer: "Well, I believe in God. Sometimes Christianity gets pretty debased, but I believe in God."

The novel *Soldiers' Pay* will furnish a good illustration of what Faulkner meant. The Episcopal clergyman in the novel is a decent and gentle man, but the loss of his son in World War I has driven him to despair. He has taken refuge from a meaningless world in cultivating his own garden, specifically an actual garden. Far from being able to give support to his flock, it is he who needs the support of others—which comes from two very unlikely good Samaritans. They probably would not claim to be Christians at all, but act with a fine impulsive kindness to help get safely home the clergyman's dazed and dying son, who had been erroneously reported missing in action. It is they and an unlettered local girl, a sort of pagan nymph, who emerge as the people able to function in a disordered and disillusioned world.

In a humble little church with a black minister and congregation, the Christian faith survives. At the end of the novel, the clergyman and his friend, on an evening walk, listen to the singing of these simple folk, and the two white men, one ostensibly a man of God, realize what they have lost. No wonder that so many readers of *Soldiers' Pay* have felt that in writing this fine first novel, Faulkner had brought T. S. Eliot's *Waste Land,* published four years earlier, out of a world-city like London into the setting of a small Southern town.

But you may ask: what has all this to do with stoicism? Just this, but I think it sufficient: the ancient Stoics at their best manifested an admirable ethical code. They insisted on the individual's responsibility for his actions. They justly earned a reputation for fortitude and courage under adversity. They even taught the brotherhood of man. It is acknowledged that they had a considerable affinity with the early Christians. Their differences from Christianity have largely to do with that they lacked: they relied on human wisdom rather than divine revelation. They lacked the doctrine of the Incarnation and any trace of Christian religious passion and fervor. The God of the Stoics was far more remote from mankind than was the Christian God. Now I am not suggesting for a moment that Faulkner ever read Zeno, Chrysippus, and Epictetus, or even the Roman Stoics like Cicero and Seneca. But he did not need to. Pantheism and stoicism are usually the first fall-back positions of Christians whose faith in revelation, the Incarnation, and the Resurrection has been weakened or lost.

Is the Reverend Mr. Mahon of Faulkner's novel a stoic? He has certainly lost all the transcendental aspects of Christianity. He tells his friend Joe Gilligan: "We make our own heaven or hell in this world." The Christian hope of an afterlife he dismisses as of no great importance. Mahon himself, however, is certainly no example of stoicism. He tells someone: "Least of all did I teach [my son] fortitude." Mahon shows little fortitude himself.

But Joe Gilligan, the rather rough-hewn returned veteran, and Margaret Powers, the good Samaritans of the novel, could fairly be called stoics. They seem pretty well bereft of Christianity; yet out of fundamental decency and kindliness they befriend the shattered and dazed young Donald Mahon and try to see his father through the ordeal of witnessing his apparently resurrected son suffer a second and real death.

I have devoted perhaps more time than I should to this first novel of Faulkner's primarily because it offers such a clear and early indication of Faulkner's cast of mind as he surveys the contemporary world. Novels like his famous *The Sound and the Fury, Light in August, Go Down, Moses,* and *Absalom, Absalom!* are far more than very promising apprentice work. They are accomplished masterpieces and offer more complex characters going through deeper moral crises. Since I cannot discuss them all in detail, I shall have to touch upon them principally for their presentation of the various shades of stoicism or warped and defective Christianity.

In *The Sound and the Fury* is depicted the downfall of the Compsons, a once distinguished family. Mr. Compson is now a defeated and despairing man. His wife is a whining and selfish woman. Their children are Quentin, a hypersensitive and self-conscious boy; Benjy, hopelessly retarded; the unspeakable Jason, crass, selfish, and brutal; and Candace, a pretty girl, vivacious, life-loving, and desperate to break away from the household. The Compson children are variously affected by the destructive influences of their parents.

For our purposes, a principal concern must be with Mr. Compson and with Quentin. Mr. Compson does try to instill in Quentin a stoic philosophy. Is Mr. Compson himself a stoic? Scarcely. He retreats too early into a reading of his dog-eared copy of Horace's verses and more often to his decanter of bourbon whiskey. He does not seriously try to save his children. Apparently he had given up long ago trying to alter his wife's conduct. It is true that he counsels his son Quentin with what may sound like stoic fortitude and patience. When Quentin comes to him in agony over what is happening to his sister Caddy, he tells Quentin that we must "stay awake and see evil done for a little while, it's not always." But even this advice is a rather debased stoicism, gained at second hand. It is not wisdom gleaned from Chrysippus or Cicero. It is from one of Faulkner's favorite poets, A. E. Housman: "Be still, be still my soul. It is but for a season, / Let us endure an hour and see injustice done."

Is Quentin himself a true stoic? I hardly think so. He is too weak and too readily brought to despair. He does act in the only way that he knows: he tries to follow the code of honor of the Old South, but is incapable of carrying it out.

His father's counsel drives him to suicide, but his death, pathetic though it is, is scarcely the protest of a Seneca, making what he regarded as the only honorable answer to a tyrant. Quentin's is an expression of weakness, not of personal strength.

As in *Soldiers' Pay,* the witness to Christianity is made by the black family, who are tenants and servants of the Compsons, and especially by Dilsey, who holds fast to her Christian faith. Dilsey comforts Benjy, tries to be a mother to Caddy, and later to Caddy's daughter. Dilsey fails, but hers is an honorable defeat.

The Compson household, it must be conceded, is a very special case. It can hardly be used to typify the weakness of a whole society or a whole tradition. But it does brilliantly set forth the quality of despair when people are bereft of any Christian hope, who, like Quentin, feel that they have no future, and who try to live by man-made codes of honor alone. Dilsey's simple faith and Caddy's genuine love for her father, for Quentin, and for Benjy set off in the sharpest possible relief the spiritual emptiness of the Compson household. About genuine faith and love Faulkner is never cynical or satirical.

I shall use *Light in August,* one of Faulkner's finest novels, to make only two points relevant to Faulkner's pull between stoicism and Christianity, but they are very important points. The first has to do with what Faulkner called the debasement of Christianity. The Reverend Mr. Mahon's tepid and essentially secularized Christianity is not the only sort that Faulkner had in mind. The other was a harsh puritanical Protestantism, which Faulkner frequently calls, somewhat unfairly perhaps, Calvinism.

The worst of these corrupters of Christianity is old Doc Hines, who worships a God of retribution and hate, actually a malignant demon, though Hines doubtless mistakes him for the Christian God. Racial bigotry has long ago devoured not only all Hines's Christian charity but even his common sense. He often speaks and acts like a madman.

Simon McEachern's puritanism takes a rather different form. He does not worship a God of hate, but a God who metes out a stern justice. McEachern tries to bring up his adopted son in the way of the Lord: In this endeavor he is obviously sincere. But he lacks kindliness, human sympathy, and mercy. Such misemphasis ends in disaster for his foster son and for McEachern himself.

The third example of a limited or perverted Christianity is the Reverend Gail Hightower. He has, in spite of his seminary training, completely missed the meaning of the Gospels. For them he has substituted an ideal of secular glory, of heroic bravery, that for Hightower has become the apex of all spirituality. In short, he lives in a dream of the past in which his idealized grandfather, a Confederate cavalry officer, dominates the whole scene. Hightower is, though he is not aware of it, utterly self-centered. He fails to give love and sympathy to his wife; and in the end he has retreated from the present world into a self-indulgent dream.

But Faulkner, I repeat, never leaves the Christian ethic utterly unrepresented. In *Light in August,* it is Byron Bunch, a methodical, hardworking, unprepossessing little man, who rides thirty miles every weekend to lead the singing in a small country church. It is he who exhibits quietly and almost apologetically what true Christian love really is. It is he who takes pity on Lena Grove when she comes into town searching for the man who fathered her child.

Faulkner often subjects those who truly attempt to lead a Christian life to the hardest tests. They must prove as tough and enduring as the stoics, but they must go further still. The case of Byron Bunch provides a good example.

Young Isaac McCaslin in *Go Down, Moses* presents another example of the difficulties encountered by such a Christian. As a boy he had been taught to love the wilderness. He had become convinced that the world of nature belongs to all mankind and that legal titles to particular tracts of land are ultimately meaningless. So when he turns twenty-one, he refuses to take possession of the great estate established by his grandfather, and his resolution is strengthened when he learns of some of the wicked actions committed by his grandfather. But in resolving to try to live, like Christ, simply by his carpenter's tools and so, in effect, to take the vow of poverty, he fails to take also the vow of chastity. Isaac wants to marry and to have a son. But his wife, who wants a home and a patrimony for her children, cannot understand his decision. She leaves him, and Ike never becomes the father he had yearned to be. Moreover, in giving up power to avoid the temptation it offers to do evil, he has by just that much weakened his power to do good in our mortal and limited actual social order. John Hunt holds that Isaac's cousin, who was next in line for the inheritance and who accepted it, better represents the conduct of the true wayfaring Christian.

Faulkner, however, treats Ike gently, but he makes clear that in his attempt to expiate family guilt, Isaac has in part ministered to his own feelings and has retreated from full engagement with the world. Our world is complicated and mysterious, too much so for our mere good intentions to set it right. A great deal has to be left up to God and God's grace. Faulkner never says this, but I think that it is implied. Like Milton, Faulkner could not praise a cloistered and fugitive virtue—though, I repeat, Faulkner respects Ike's motives and his noble intentions.

Faulkner seems to be clearly aware of a distinction between the Stoic virtues and what a Christian adds, or ought to add, to them. For him, one proof that courage and fortitude are not enough is shown in his treatment of his sternly "Calvinist" characters. Surely, a Simon McEachern has plenty of fortitude in following his convictions, and a Gail Hightower shows a certain bravery. He will not leave town when his parishioners advise it; he will not be browbeaten by public opinion; he will not compromise with his vision of glory and his chosen way of life. But McEachern lacks magnanimity and charity, and so finally does Hightower.

Faulkner valued courage. A coward was of no use to God or man. He also valued fortitude. These are the qualities of Faulkner's most interesting characters. I have in mind Joe Christmas of *Light in August*, and Thomas Sutpen of *Absalom, Absalom!*. Both are paragons of courage and endurance, and Faulkner expects us to see both of them as truly men of great stature. But Joe Christmas stretches the bonds of human nature until they almost snap, rejecting the human community, all womankind, and even nature itself; and Thomas Sutpen, in the pursuit of his fanatical ambition to establish what amounts to a baronial estate and found a dynasty, becomes finally inhuman, destroying his wife and his children and at last being himself destroyed by a tenant whom he has injured.

Some account of Sutpen will allow me to make another important point: Faulkner never confuses his stoicism with Gnosticism, an ancient heresy which in our time, with renewed strength, exalts man and in effect allows him to take the place of God. Some of our most profound thinkers see it as our great present danger. Obviously Sutpen never heard of Gnosticism, nor, I dare say, had Faulkner. But that doesn't matter. In our brilliant technological age, in which man visibly remakes nature, goes into outer space, explores the moon, and has achieved the power to wipe out civilization itself, it's natural for a new *hubris* to develop. Man is not only the measure of all things, as some of the ancient Greeks thought, but is now, or soon will be, the master of all things, and if not to become the creator, at least be able to recreate—to mold things closer to his heart's desire.

Sutpen is the perfect example of the American self-made man. He rises, by his own energy and power, from rags to great riches. He comes to believe that he can do anything. He admits that he occasionally makes a mistake, but mistakes can be corrected. He is certain that he makes only mistakes; the word *sin* is not in his vocabulary.

For example, one of his mistakes was to marry in Haiti a planter's daughter, who turned out to have a trace of African blood. When he discovers it, he concludes that she will not fit into his grand design. True, her trace of African blood is so small that it will never be apparent and only he will know it. Moreover, Sutpen, it turns out, has little racial prejudice himself. The fact that he will know is enough to disqualify her. And so he abandons her and his young son and emigrates to Mississippi.

Sutpen works entirely in terms of blueprints, schedules, and timetables. He has a boundless confidence in his ability to solve any problem. He has no need of God, and no place to put Him in his scheme of things.

The heroic quality in Sutpen is that he never gives up. Nevertheless, Sutpen is revealed to be finally guileless, a true innocent. He has never come to understand the true nature of reality. For Sutpen, reality lacks any mystery; it is only a complex mechanism. He is sure that, given time, he will be able to master all its workings.

In his answers to questions, in his interviews, and most notably in his famous Nobel Prize speech, Faulkner praises man and keeps telling us that man will endure and furthermore that he will "prevail." Such statements may appear to prove that Faulkner himself believes in man's own self-sufficiency. Not so. To prove this, we do not have to rely merely on Faulkner's treatment of Sutpen and other such characters. He has told us that he believes in a Creator God, and as for man's solving all his problems, Faulkner said to one of his interviewers: "Granted time," man will solve most of his problems "except the problems that he is doomed forever to, simply because he is flesh and blood." In short, Faulkner sees man not as a demi-god but as a mortal creature, limited by his mortal condition.

I obviously am in rather close agreement with Hunt's thesis about Faulkner's ultimate beliefs. But I do have some reservations about one of his statements, namely, that Southern society was basically stoic in its beliefs. I think that there is some truth in this view, but I would like to enter a few qualifications.

In the first place, one must not forget the strength of the evangelical churches in the nineteenth-century South. Remember, too, the revival meetings with their ecstatic outpourings of emotion and their emphasis, in hymn and sermon, on the saving blood of Jesus. The religion of the Southern folk was not diluted by a rationalistic quasi-deism. It was ardent and passionate and had not lost its transcendental element. In fact, the only segment of the Southern society for which the claim of stoicism can be made is the Southern plantation gentry, and this group was numerically small, though politically and socially powerful. Even with this group, one has to use caution: there are just too many obvious exceptions.

It is true that the Virginian Founding Fathers were influenced by the writings of the Roman Stoics, and Thomas Jefferson gives them credit for moving away from the supernatural trappings of Christianity toward the reasonable beliefs of deism. But even in colonial Virginia the religion of the planter class was more conventionally orthodox than that. The typical parishioner was hostile to anything that smacked of "papacy." Moreover, he was fearful of giving too much power to the bishops, and so was typically a rather tepid, easygoing low-church Episcopalian. He did not trouble his head much about theology. But I don't see him as particularly stoical. The truth is that Saint John the

Divine in the Book of Revelation has provided us with a more accurate term: Laodicean. In Chapter 3, verses 15–16, the church at Laodicea is described as neither hot nor cold, just lukewarm. Saint John obviously couldn't give very high marks to this congregation. On reflection, however, I believe it would be quite unrealistic to claim that the only habitat of the Laodicean was the Old South. I dare say he or she exists in present-day churches all over the United States.

Yet even lukewarm Christians get their standards from somewhere. They are too conventional to adopt radically new standards of conduct or newfangled beliefs. So with the Laodiceans of the Southern gentry who do occur in Faulkner's novels. They had their codes of conduct and manners to which the best of them adhered about as well as any other such class had done, and that code was not incompatible with Christianity. But like any code of manners and indeed any purely secular code, it did not go far enough. Thus, it is not sufficient that a gentleman simply knows, by instinct or breeding, what a gentleman can do and not do, or that a lady should need no instruction in what ladylike behavior is. I grant that the atmosphere of a tightly cohesive society in which people do not have to be constantly told what is proper and what is not may seem refreshing to those who are constantly needing to consult Ann Landers or the marriage counselor, since they seem to have no standards of their own.

Nevertheless, we must admit that those who believe that inherited social codes are enough are living on the moral capital stored up by their forefathers. In time, that capital, unless renewed, is bound to run out. This is, in effect, the view of a number of more recent Southern poets and novelists. I have in mind here such writers as Allen Tate, Flannery O'Connor, and Walker Percy.

In Walker Percy's *Lost in the Cosmos,* there is a hilarious takeoff on a typical Phil Donahue TV show: for instance, the matter for discussion is the case of Penny, a teenaged unwed expectant mother. Dr. Joyce Friday, celebrated sex expert is there; Penny's proud parents; and, of course, Penny herself, who has conceived the child because she thinks "babies are neat." But in the midst of Donahue's characteristic handling of the case, in walk three uninvited visitors: John Calvin, clad in his black Geneva gown; a young man wearing a Confederate uniform; and a Cosmic Stranger from outer space. It is, however, only with the second visitor that we are concerned here.

Donahue rises to the occasion and, without turning a hair, brings all three into his act. Here is his colloquy with the young Confederate officer.

DONAHUE *(holding mike to the officer)*: How about you, sir? Your name is—

CONFEDERATE OFFICER: Colonel John Pelham, C.S.A., commander of the horse artillery under General Stuart.

PENNY: He's cute.

AUDIENCE: *(Laughter)*

DONAHUE: You heard it all in the green room, Colonel. What d'ya think?

COLONEL PELHAM *(in a soft Alabama accent)*: What do I think of what, sir?

DONAHUE: Of what you heard in the green room.

PELHAM: Of the way these folks act and talk? Well, I don't think much of it, sir.

DONAHUE: How do you mean, Colonel?

PELHAM: That's not the way people should talk or act. Where I come from, we'd call them white trash. That's no way to talk if you're a man or a woman. A gentleman knows how to treat women. He knows because he knows himself, who he is, what his obligations are. And he discharges them. But after all, you won the war, so if that's the way you want to act, that's your affair. At least, we can be sure of one thing.

DONAHUE: What's that, Colonel?

PELHAM: We're not sorry we fought.

DONAHUE: I see. Then you agree with the reverend. I mean, Reverend Calvin here.

PELHAM: Well, I respect his religious beliefs. But I never thought much about religion one way or the other.

One could scarcely ask for a more precise illustration of a social class that has little interest in theology or even religion, but lives by nature and custom. Representatives of this class are to be found in Walker Percy's other novels. They have admirable traits, and obviously Percy finds young Colonel Pelham attractive and means for his reader to find him so. But Percy's criticism of the spiritual inadequacy of this class is not, of course, altered. Characters of this general sort occur in Faulkner too. Even so, we must be careful not to take the case too far. For in the very army in which Pelham fought were Generals Lee and Jackson, whose religious convictions were very strong.

Let me return, however, specifically to Faulkner. The gentry in his novels tend to look down on the more extreme evangelistic sects. But Faulkner himself has written some highly sympathetic accounts of the pastors of such congregations, both white and black. In *The Unvanquished*, it is Brother Fortinbride who takes over—obviously with the community's approval—the funeral service for the beloved Mrs. Rosa Millard, even though Mrs. Compson and some of the town ladies had provided what they thought was a more dignified minister. As Faulkner tells the story, it is Brother Fortinbride who speaks with the voice of earned authority—not the citified pastor.

I must not conclude, however, without making one last attempt to clarify the difference between stoicism and what I shall call Gnosticism, that heresy which may have become the most threatening intellectual aberration of our time. I want also to provide a clear example of what John Hunt meant by "Stoic Christianity." For the best illustrations I need turn back to what I regard as probably Faulkner's greatest novel, *Absalom, Absalom!*.

Earlier I dealt with the character of Thomas Sutpen, the self-made man, the poor mountain boy who resolves to beat the Virginia Tidewater aristocrats at their own game. Is he a stoic in Hunt's terms? He has self-reliance, courage, and fortitude in abundance, and these are Stoic virtues. Many readers have wanted to see in Sutpen the typical Southern plantation owner. For them, he is the Southern Stoic in the highest degree.

But General Compson, for example, is much more representative of the Southern gentry. He may lack something of Sutpen's tremendous vitality, but he also lacks his towering ambition. Whether he has large resources of residual Christianity or simply a nurturing in the basic human decencies, he recognizes something terribly wrong in Sutpen's inhuman dedication to his design. Sutpen tells him that he had to abandon his wife and son back in Haiti, but that he has satisfied his own conscience in the matter, since he has made a full and even generous money settlement of any claims that his wife might suppose she had on him. General Compson fairly explodes with shock and disbelief. He asks Sutpen what kind of conscience he has that "would warrant [him] in the belief that [he] could have bought immunity from [her] for no other coin than justice." The cash nexus does not apply to matters of love and trust.

I call Sutpen a Gnostic because of his willingness to abolish any ethical standard that contradicts his own will to power. We have seen a great deal of this in our own troubled century. It is not a regional problem—and certainly not that of an old-fashioned conservative society—but it is a national and international problem. Faulkner is not merely a Southern writer. If the South is the usual setting for his fiction, the issues with which he deals are universal problems and present dangers.

Sutpen treats his wives and his children as merely pawns in his power game. He clearly destroys his two sons. But his daughter Judith could not be utterly destroyed. Something wonderful survived. She inherited her father's powerful will and his ability to handle any hardship. But she added the love and compassion that he utterly lacked.

Some readers have felt that Judith proved a rather cold and comfortless foster mother to the bewildered little boy that she brought to live with her. But then what do they expect? Pollyanna, all smiles in a cheap gingham dress though worn out after plowing all day as she tries to grow food for them to eat?

Judith, brought up so delicately to be the chatelaine of a great estate, had seen her fiancé killed at the very plantation gate, by her own brother, for reasons unaccountable to her. The iron had indeed entered her soul. Faulkner as an artist who believed in telling the truth about human beings would not have honored his truth if he had not depicted Judith as she was and as she must have appeared to a little boy suddenly uprooted from his New Orleans home. But the sensitive reader will also be aware of the essential goodness and kindness as well as the courage of this woman, still young, but gaunt with poverty and backbreaking work.

I promised a clear example of John Hunt's phrase "Stoic Christianity." I have just given it: Judith Sutpen herself.

Faulkner
and the
American Dream

The post–Nobel Prize book of Faulkner's that I have undertaken to discuss may seem a strange choice, for it is a book that was never completed. Nevertheless, I think it is worthy of discussion. It can tell us a good deal about the later Faulkner and about what, toward the end of his days, he thought of American society.

The circumstances that prompted him to project such a book might make some of us from the very start question its value. Was the projected book really any more than an outburst of hurt feelings over a personal incident? Could even a writer as talented as Faulkner have inflated a relatively trivial incident into a convincing example of the failure of the American dream of freedom?

It may be just as well to rehearse the circumstances that set him off. *Life* magazine decided to make Faulkner the subject of a full-dress article which eventually appeared in two parts in the issues for September 18 and October 5 of 1953.

When Faulkner got wind of what was up, he tried to stop it and, of course, failed. Later in October, 1953, he wrote to his friend Phillip Mullen: "I tried for years to prevent this sort of thing, asked them to let me alone. It is too bad that the individual in this country has no protection from journalism." Since a man's private life could be in-

Given as a lecture, entitled "Faulkner's *The American Dream*: What Happened to It?," at the 1985 international Faulkner conference in Ito, Japan.

vaded over his protest and plea, no wonder that people "in the rest of the world don't like us, since we seem to have neither taste nor courtesy, and know and believe in nothing but money and it doesn't matter how you get it."

This is indeed a bitter indictment. Did Faulkner overreact? Or was his outburst one of justified indignation? In any case, his was an odd response, and he knew it was, for some millions of Americans would do anything short of a criminal act to gain so much free publicity as a full-dress exposure in *Life* afforded. Faulkner raised no objection to other writers receiving this kind of attention, provided they had no objection. He didn't begrudge it to Hemingway, for example. He simply did not want it for himself and did not see why he didn't have a right to refuse it.

Faulkner's concern for privacy apparently did not spring from a fear that certain discreditable episodes in his own life might be revealed. The journalist who wrote the article, Robert Coughlan, was not bent upon an exposé and pulled no skeletons out of the closet. Joseph Blotner points out that Coughlan actually "de-emphasized some of the comments that Faulkner had received, including a harsh and extended critique of the man and his work from Phil Stone."

Since Faulkner's death some of his friends and intimate acquaintances have published accounts that reveal far more of unconventional, bohemian, or other behavior likely to offend the censorious. Such evidence then suggests to me that Faulkner was not worried about discreditable revelations, but that he honestly felt that an important principle was at stake.

In discussing the proper limits of journalism, Faulkner was careful to make a distinction between a man's private life and his public life. By selling his work for publication, Faulkner conceded that he had opened the door to criticism of it. But he held that his private life was quite another matter. His exact words are: "Until the writer [has] committed a crime or run for public office, his private life [is] his own."

Whether Faulkner's distinction between public and private can be successfully maintained in the practical world of today is far from certain. T. S. Eliot, for example, directed that his literary executrix and his publisher render no aid toward the publication of his biography. But an authorized biography nevertheless is, I have been told, now planned in order to counteract the unauthorized biographies that have appeared, not to mention a play such as *Tom and Viv*. But the point here is not whether Faulkner's distinction can be maintained, but that Faulkner felt that it ought to be.

At any rate, Faulkner quickly decided to speak out on the subject. By late October of 1954 he had written to his editor, Saxe Commins, that he had sent him a rewritten version of what he called his "Freedom of Press" article, and went on to say that on reflection he now saw it was just one "section of a kind of symposium [comprising] maybe 5 or 6 lectures, on *The American Dream: What Happened to It?*." He thought, however, that it might become "a book later, on what has happened to the American Dream which at one time the whole earth looked up, aspired to."

What Faulkner had sent to Commins was the essay "On Privacy," which *Harper's* published in July, 1955. Only one other section of his ambitious project was ever published, "On Fear: The South in Labor." It too was published by *Harper's,* in June, 1956. Faulkner did give parts of the essay "On Fear" as a lecture in various places: at the University of Montana, to an audience in Manila, to another in Memphis, Tennessee, and to one in Japan. In a letter of July, 1955, he wrote that he might even compose a third lecture on his general subject, one specifically for reading in Japan. But he did not do so, and somewhere about this time the original proposal seems to have guttered out.

Although we have only a fragment—perhaps a third of Faulkner's book on the failure of the American Dream—the two completed essays have much to tell us about Faulkner's ideas and attitudes toward American culture and American history, especially the ideas and attitudes that he had come to hold seven years before his death. A closer examination of "On Privacy" may even suggest the issues he might have addressed in the three or four chapters that he never got down on paper. For, as we have seen, in this impassioned essay "On Privacy," he is consciously attempting to ground his personal case on principles that he regarded as those of the Founding Fathers of the Republic.

What about the second of the chapters that Faulkner did write, "On Fear"? Does it also bear on his troubled concern about what had happened to the American Dream? It does, but I shall say less about this essay because its connection with the failure of the American Dream is so obvious. What Faulkner stated in it he believed then needed to be said to his fellow Mississippians and other Southerners, but it hardly requires being restated here.

To be brief, then: withholding from the black people of their full civil rights, and specifically forcing them into segregated schools, Faulkner saw as a flagrant denial of the opening sentence of the Declaration of Independence. As we know, Jefferson himself was troubled by that contradiction, and explicitly referred to it on a number of later occasions. The Civil War had freed the black man from his state of being a slave, but there had been no serious or sustained effort to give him his full civil rights. After nearly a century of neglect on the part of American society generally, there was a lot of unfinished business, and Faulkner asked the South now to put its own house in order, specifically with the elimination of segregated schools.

Whatever some may be tempted to allege with regard to Faulkner's defense of his privacy, few would argue that this chapter on freedom for the black man is peevishly self-serving, for it brought down on him recriminations from fellow Southerners, from his friends, and even from members of his own family circle. It cost Faulkner something.

How Jeffersonian both of these published essays are. The concept of freedom for the individual is central to both. Moreover, a careful reading of "On Fear" will indicate that the principles invoked there are thoroughly consistent with those upon which the essay "On Privacy" is based.

In describing what had happened to the American Dream, Faulkner speaks more in sorrow than in anger. In this account of his native region, the South, Faulkner spoke out against its delinquencies because he loved it. The rest of the country has emphatically approved of Faulkner's willingness to point out the faults of his own region; but the rest of America must be prepared to hear him address what he saw as the failures of American society in general. With it too he had a lover's quarrel. He believed that he was reproving it for its own good.

What circumstances had brought about this invasion of privacy? A corporation's desire to make money by whatever means. Faulkner was a realist. No one had to tell him about the value of money. Through most of his life, money was for him in chronically short supply. Moreover, he knew that cupidity had from the beginning been man's prime temptation. Holy Writ puts it this way: "The love of money is the root of all evil." Nevertheless, all civilized societies of various times in the past counted it dishonorable to stoop to certain ways of gaining money.

Faulkner evidently believed that in an earlier day American society looked askance at the invasion of privacy. I shall leave it to the professional historians to judge the accuracy of this statement, but Faulkner clearly believed that a deterioration of morals and manners had occurred. Specifically, there had been a letdown in courage, honor, pride, and humility.

This is a serious charge, but Faulkner had for a long time believed that there had been some such deterioration. He had not had to wait until 1953 to discover the fact. As early as 1946 he had written to Lambert Davis: "There are times when I believe there has been little in this country since . . . 1860–70, etc. good enough to make good literature, that since then we have gradually become a nation of bragging sentimental not too courageous liars. We seem to be losing all confidence not only in our national character but in man's integrity too."

This is exactly the tone of Roth Edmonds's bitter comments on American attitudes toward democracy and patriotism in "Delta Autumn." Roth asks his companions how they expect Americans to stop Hitler: "By singing God Bless America in bars at midnight and wearing dime-store flags in our lapels?" Uncle Ike makes it very plain that he had not given up hope in the patriotism and essential decency of the American people. Nor did Faulkner ever give up hope in them or in the human race itself. He believed that mankind would somehow survive and even "prevail," as he had said in his Nobel Prize speech. Nevertheless, Roth Edmonds gives expression here to what was evidently, from time to time, Faulkner's own anxiety.

At any rate, in 1955, Faulkner writes that the degeneration had arisen at that "moment in our history when we decided that the old simple moral verities . . . were obsolete and to be discarded." His calling them "old" indicates that he was thinking of the traditional values of the kind that the whole community had long accepted. Faulkner attached great importance to the community. That he did so is evident from its presence in his stories and novels as a powerful force.

The truth is that it is necessary to have a community if you are to have true individualism. Faulkner may have grasped this fact only instinctively, but it has been spelled out for us in a book which Faulkner never read. I refer to Richard N. Goodwin's *American Condition* (1974). Goodwin, a New Englander, was one of President Kennedy's speechwriters.

Like Faulkner, Goodwin describes American society as suffering from "a lack of discipline, of sanctions, of community values, and a sense of mission." In it "the individual has lost his relation to society," and Goodwin insists that true freedom to be oneself depends upon the fact of a community based upon shared values. He points out that with the loss of community, "inner constraints" are also lost, and the state has to regulate conduct by force, with a concomitant reduction "of the power and freedom of the individual."

Notice that even in his essay "On Privacy," Faulkner's thinking approximates Goodwin's. What had happened to him had to be ascribed to a whole system—to what the society had become—and not to personal malice of particular individuals. Thus, he doesn't blame Coughlan, the writer of the *Life* article. For had he refused to write it, he would have been fired, and someone else would have been assigned. Even the publishers were not acting vindictively toward him. A corporation is expected to make money for its stockholders. If an article on Faulkner promised to increase sales, what else was the corporation expected to do?

Faulkner described the situation: "The three of us (I, the journalist, and the publisher) were faced as one not with an idea, a principle of choice between good and evil . . . but with a fact, a condition of our American life before which all three of us were (at that moment) helpless."

Even so, we all want to justify what we are doing. And so language itself suffers debasement as corporation lawyers, politicians, and journalists turn out phrases like "freedom of the press" or "national security" to sanction the invasion of the privacy of an individual. Language in such cases is, of course, being used dishonestly, and the debasement of language, Faulkner properly realized, is a serious matter indeed. Among others in our time, George Orwell and Denis de Rougemont have addressed the topic in books that have become celebrated. The degeneration goes on: in an age in which the ghostwriter, the PR man, and the advertising expert have become more and more the movers and shakers of society, we are already feeling the effects of language used to manipulate and sometimes with the express purpose of deception.

Yet what I have thus far discussed hardly does justice to Faulkner's attempt to show that democracy as expressed in the Declaration of Independence and in the Constitution, by implication at least, protects the privacy of the individual. For Faulkner attempts to put the current invasions of privacy into a historical context.

In the Old World and in an older day the mere individual counted for little unless he was a nobleman, a churchman high in the ecclesiastical establishment, or a fighting man of notable abilities. The men and women who made up the rest of the population amounted to little in their own right: they were *subjects*. The American Dream held out the hope that every individual might be freed from mere subjecthood and given the opportunity to become a complete person and given, with the vote, the power of choosing who were to be the officers of the state.

Granted that this dream was never fully realized, but a worthy attempt had been made to bring it to fruition. Jefferson, for example, not only declared that freedom and power of choice were individual rights but wanted to go further and guarantee the right of every individual to receive from the state at least a basic education and the ownership of enough land to render him economically independent and thus able to cast an honest vote. Such was the Jeffersonian American Dream and, as we have seen, such was essentially Faulkner's.

Now, however, as Faulkner saw it, the individual person was in danger of being pressed down once more into the undifferentiated mass, with no special character of his own. This is what I make of Faulkner's wonderfully contorted rhetoric as he described what the American Dream had held out to the masses of Europe: "There is room . . . all ye individually homeless, individually oppressed, individually unindividualized." In America their God-given but latent individuality was to be redeemed, their dignity as persons in their own right, and, as a necessary part of it, their privacy.

Let me say here that I think that Thomas Jefferson, under the influence of the Enlightenment, was somewhat naïve in trusting so much in man's natural goodness, and that he conveniently forgot how much man's inalienable rights owed to the Christian theologians of the despised Middle Ages. Perhaps Faulkner himself expected rather too much of man in his own nature. Nevertheless, the dream was a noble one, and Faulkner's indignation at what he believed had happened to it is worthy of our respect.

Yet probably more than Jefferson, Faulkner was aware of his debt to the special culture in which he had been brought up. He had grown up in a true community, a society bound together by more than merely economic ties. The "old verities" had survived. Manners and morals did not need to be debated. In speaking of the South to an interviewer in 1952, Faulkner said: "It's the only really authentic region in the United States, because a deep indestructible bond still exists between man and his environment. In the South, above all, there is still a common acceptance of the world, a common view of life, and a common morality." Ladies and gentlemen knew from their very nurture what was decent behavior and what was not.

It was also a society in which men were sensitive—often hypersensitive—to any impugnment of their personal honor. Dueling lasted longer in the South than anywhere else in the United States, and as late as the 1850s a book outlining the code duello was published in Charleston, South Carolina.

Loyalty to the community and patriotism with regard to the nation seemed almost instinctive. That could prove a weakness. No wonder that Walker Percy sees the Old South, for all its admirable virtues, paying too little attention to theology and relying too heavily on inherited manners and decorum.

Faulkner was not, of course, blind to the faults of the small-town Southern community: its racial prejudices—witness his essay "On Fear"—but also its parochialism, its distrust of outsiders, and its fundamentalist hot-gospeling evangelists. He had been annoyed at being dismissed as a scoutmaster because he enjoyed his beer; and like most literary artists, he had his bohemian streak and bitterly resented dogmatic puritanism. In his novels he takes due notice of these qualities in such characters as Joe Christmas's foster father, Simon McEachern, and Joe's crazed grandfather, old Doc Hines.

Yet what Faulkner saw arising in twentieth-century America was something that appeared to him much more ominous. In sensing these threats, he was very close to writers on the international scene such as T. S. Eliot, W. B. Yeats, and Franz Kafka. Yet some may wonder at my placing Faulkner in such company. True, like Yeats, he had some experience of a landed society with its attendant peasantry, and he shared something of Eliot's deeply grounded conservatism, but could he be said to share their international view? Wasn't he just an old-fashioned Southerner, hopelessly behind the times and too much blinkered by his provincialism to be able to make any useful and perceptive criticism of the centralized, highly industrialized culture of modern America?

The best refutation of such a view is to compare Faulkner's criticism of present-day American culture with that of critics who come out of a very different kind of tradition. I have already mentioned Richard Goodwin. Let me adduce another witness, Christopher Lasch, born in 1932 in the Midwest, and now a professor of history at the University of Rochester. Among other works, he is the author of *The New Radicalism in America,* a title that doesn't sound very Faulknerian. If we are looking for a man opposite to Faulkner by tradition and nurture, Lasch seems to fit the bill almost perfectly. Consider his *Culture of Narcissism* (1978).

The title of the first chapter of that book includes the significant phrase "the social invasion of the self." Lasch takes the general invasion of the self in our society to be an even more serious matter than Faulkner had in "On Privacy." Lasch's account of how this invasion came about also curiously resembles Faulkner's. He writes: "Most of the evils discussed in this book originate in a new kind of paternalism, which has risen from the ruins of the old paternalism of kings, priests, and authoritarian fathers, slave masters and land overlords. . . . Today this priestly and monarchial hegemony [has been replaced] with the hegemony of the business corporation, the managerial and professional classes who operate the corporate system, and the corporate state." This account almost exactly parallels Faulkner's opening remarks in "On Privacy." Faulkner there described the American Dream as having promised "a sanctuary on the earth for individual man," a sanctuary in which man could be free "of the old established closed-corporation hierarchies of arbitrary power . . . of church and state." Faulkner went on to write that we had indeed shaken off the rule of royal and ecclesiastical overlords, but now we were about to lose that hard-won freedom and individuality to the soulless corporation.

Even in his interpretation of the Civil War, Lasch is not wholly unlike Faulkner. Lasch writes that the democratic revolution of the eighteenth and early nineteenth centuries which culminated in the Civil War "not only did away with monarchy but undermined established religion, landed elites, and finally overthrew the slaveholding oligarchy of the South." But what then developed, Lasch says, was "a society based on individualism, competition, and the pursuit of the main chance." In short, what followed was the Gilded Age, the robber barons, and the degradation of what for Lasch should have been the proper democratic socialist society, or in Faulkner's different and simpler terms, the breakdown of the American Dream.

In considering the last quotation from Lasch, we should not, by the way, let his use of the term *individualism* confuse the issue. Lasch does not mean by it precisely what Faulkner means—personal freedom, liberty to realize one's full being. For example, Lasch writes that American capitalism had resulted in the decline of individualism, which has nowadays degenerated into what Lasch calls "narcissism." Narcissistic man is no longer vigorous economic man. He is haunted by anxiety, unsure of himself, and more and more dependent on the state. Consciously or unconsciously, he is content with the new paternalism. Hence the title Lasch chose for his book, *The Culture of Narcissism.*

In their visions of what American society ought to be today, Lasch and Faulkner obviously differ, as one would expect them to, but even here there are likenesses. Faulkner would surely have approved of Lasch's recommendation that in the future the citizen should rely more on his personal judgment and common sense and less on the advice of state-sponsored "experts"; and Lasch's emphasis on localism would have warmed the states' rights cockles of Faulkner's heart. But my present concern is not with their agreement on what America ought to be but with their judgments of America's defects.

Both Faulkner and Lasch are much concerned with the modern loosening of family ties, the erosion of the sense of community, and—here I shall use Lasch's own words—the "atrophy of older traditions of self-help [which] has ended everyday competence in one area after another and has made the individual dependent on the state, the corporation, and other bureaucracies."

Both men deplore the modern dismissal of the past. Lasch sees the "past as a political and psychological treasury from which we draw the reserves . . . that we need to cope with the future." I hardly need to quote from Faulkner on this point: *Flags in the Dust, The Unvanquished, Absalom, Absalom!, The Reivers,* and many other of his novels reveal how heavily Faulkner draws on the past as a source of wisdom in its account of human triumph and failure.

Rather surprisingly, both men have a good word to say for religion. Lasch, along with Freud, regards religion as an illusion, and Faulkner was scarcely the orthodox churchman. But Faulkner was aware of the painful loss of what he called the "old verities," and Lasch notes that the fading of religion has left a void that has not been filled. Lasch ranks religion, along with compassion and contemplative reason, as the source of "the standards that would condemn crime or cruelty."

He points out that "in a society that has reduced reason to mere calculation, [such] reason can impose no limits on the . . . immediate
gratification of every desire, no matter how perverse, insane, criminal,
or merely immoral." Now in our present society, Lasch writes, "there
is no logical place for religion, compassion, or contemplative reason."
That fact is ominous.

I trust that I have shown enough to dispose of the notion that
Faulkner's essay "On Privacy" simply expressed the disgruntlement of
an old-fashioned Southerner whose standards of conduct are hopelessly outmoded. It is obvious that acute contemporary critics of American society who come out of a radically different intellectual climate
can make judgments that are, at point after point, surprisingly close to
Faulkner's own. In fact, even on the specific circumstances that trig-
gered Faulkner's outburst in his essay "On Privacy"—even on these—
Lasch's position is close to Faulkner's own. On the obliteration of the
boundaries between the public and the private world, Lasch writes:

> People with narcissistic personalities . . . play a conspicuous part in con-
> temporary life, often rising to positions of eminence. Thriving on the
> adulation of the masses, these celebrities set the tone of public life and pri-
> vate life as well, since the machinery of celebrity recognizes no boundaries
> between the public and private realm. The beautiful people—to use this
> revealing expression to include not merely wealthy globetrotters but all
> those who bask . . . in the full glare of the cameras—live out the fantasy of
> narcissistic success, which consists of nothing more substantial than a wish
> to be vastly admired, not for one's accomplishments but simply for oneself,
> uncritically and without reservation.

Faulkner refused to be one of the "beautiful" people. He had no
wish to be one of those macho personalities such as a Hemingway or a
Mailer. He was justly proud of his accomplishments and was willing
for them to be judged critically. But he was bent on keeping his private
life separate from his public life. Yet even in his essay "On Privacy," he
sensed the hopelessness of his plight. He was not dealing with a real
person but with a corporation and finally with modern American society itself.

In my own opinion Faulkner could easily have filled up the three or
four additional essays that he had told Commins he intended to write.
I have an idea that one of them might well have been entitled "On

Respectability." Respectability was Faulkner's special bête noir. Remember, in *The Wild Palms,* the wonderful tirade of Harry Wilbourne on respectability. Remember too that it was this snare in which even Flem Snopes finally became entangled. But it is pointless to speculate further on the probable topics of the unwritten essays. It is enough to say that Faulkner had plenty of material on the failure of the American Dream.

Yet I do not regret that he left those essays unwritten. I am content that his later energies went into fiction, the thing that he did best and that we cherish most. Yet speculation on what Faulkner might have added to his unfinished book is not unprofitable. Clearly, Faulkner had thought deeply and coherently about the forces at work in American society. They were forces that he foresaw would inevitably impinge upon his own native region.

And what about Faulkner's stance as a Southerner? Any thoughtful reader of Faulkner's fiction becomes aware that he believed that the South was significantly different from the rest of the country. He also believed that these differences were centuries old. A novel like *Intruder in the Dust* (1949) indicates that he regarded the differences as still powerful as late as mid-century. What Gavin Stevens says on the subject in this novel and what Chick Mallison felt are expressions, I am convinced, of Faulkner's own beliefs and feelings. There is plenty of corroborative evidence.

As a critic of what was happening to American culture, Faulkner found that his strong regional consciousness proved to be no handicap. He was enabled to view the cultural scene both as an insider and as an outsider. The special angle of vision that double role afforded him provided its own degree of truth.

Faulkner
and
History

A people without history
Is not redeemed from time, for history is a pattern
Of timeless moments.
—T. S. Eliot

. . . the dream of the future is not
Better than the fact of the past, no matter how terrible.
For without the fact of the past we cannot dream the future.
—R. P. Warren

Faulkner's novels are drenched in history and his most thoughtful characters frequently speculate about its meaning. Such speculations, either as voiced by one of the characters or merely implied by the tenor of the novel, make it plain that Faulkner's historical concern is much more than an amiable antiquarianism. Consider *Absalom, Absalom!*. Even though there are costumes aplenty in it, no one in his right mind would confuse it with mere costume romance. Yet William Faulkner's conception of history can stand further attention than it commonly receives. A meaningful account of it, however, will require some comment on the concept of nature and of human nature that his notion of history implies.

Given as a lecture at the 1971 South Central Modern Language Association meeting in New Orleans, and originally published in slightly different form in *Mississippi Quarterly,* XXV (Spring, 1972, Supplement). Used with permission.

As for nature, Faulkner's interest in it is almost as deep and as pervasive as is his interest in human action. Nature as constituting the arena in which man operates and as a factor in constantly qualifying all human action simply cannot be separated from history itself. Yet Faulkner's nature is not simply a necessary evil—something to be manipulated—an obstruction to man's purposes that on occasion has to be bulldozed out of the way or else raw material that has to be shaped into a house or a piece of furniture to serve man's purposes. Nature at once nourishes man and challenges him; but it has its own life apart from his, which means that he can never fully control it. Man has a history, but nature has no history; its changes are illusory, merely seasonal or cyclical. Nature through all its changes is immortal.

In nature's depths there lurks a numinous quality that man must respect, even fear, and ought to come to love. Faulkner's villains do not respect nature and their fear of it has nothing in common with the fear of the Lord or with awe in the presence of the divine. Rather, it is typified in Popeye's instinctive revulsion from what is not merely mechanical. He is afraid to walk through a clump of trees. The swoop of an owl terrifies him.

How are history and nature related? We can learn a great deal about any writer's conception of reality by noticing how he relates them—if, in fact, he can find any relation between them. In more recent decades, with the breakup of the Christian synthesis, nature and history have tended to fall apart, and some of our writers stress one at the expense of the other, or simply convert one into an aspect of the other.

It may save time and clear the air if I give a brief résumé of the Christian synthesis. Man and nature were both created by a good and loving God. They are therefore essentially good, and in the Garden story, Adam lives in a happy rapport with nature. But man in his presumptuous pride broke his relation to God and with it his rapport with nature. He invented fire, tools, and a technology, and began to prey on nature. Yet though it was now impossible for him to fall back into the old harmony with nature, as an act of grace God did make it possible for man to achieve salvation and to be reunited with Him. But not in the realm of nature and not in the world of history and time.

With the waning of Christianity, man no longer glories in having been made in the image of God, but takes his place as merely the wisest of the beasts. He can use his reason and his consciousness to make himself master of nature and, as our more optimistic thinkers would have it, to control his own destiny and to write his own history. This perhaps is the dominant tendency in our time, but among the artists, including the literary artists, we have seen a strong countertendency: man's subjection of nature, including the pressures that he puts on his own human nature, is decried. Man needs, D. H. Lawrence would say, to yield to nature once more, to give himself up to its rhythms, to cultivate his own instinctive and spontaneous impulses, and, in short, to return to ancient pastoral poetry and to revive the old pagan gods.

I am conscious that in saying this, I am oversimplifying scandalously; yet if I am to say anything to the purpose about Faulkner and history, I must rely on schematic outlines.

It is with the dominant tendency that I shall be primarily concerned—with those thinkers who believe that man can determine his own history. They tend to be utopians or millennialists, and this streak of millennialism runs very powerfully through our culture. We find it at the very beginning of our history and in an almost classic form in the Puritans of New England. These were a dedicated people, the militant left wing of Protestantism, who meant to return to God's plan as set forth in the Scriptures, and to establish the New Jerusalem, the divine society as ordained by God, on the soil of the New World.

The New England Puritans were of course sufficiently orthodox not to presume that man was perfectible or that all the human miseries, including sickness, old age, and death, could be done away with. They still held firmly to the doctrine of Original Sin. They had no illusions that they could restore man to his immortal state, living once more in the happy garden of an unfallen nature. Yet as the doctrine of Original Sin faded, and as man's powers to control nature increased, the millennial ideal gradually became secularized. The Puritan determination to build the perfect society, far from weakening, was simply redirected from the eternal to the temporal, from the City of Heaven to an earthly city of the here and now.

Saint Augustine, in his famous discussion of the City of God and the city of man, certainly expected the Christian to use the heavenly city as the model for his earthly enterprise, but he made it plain that it could not be built through man's efforts, but only by God's grace, and in God's own good time. In fact, whenever it was achieved, time would be at an end and the citizens of this New Jerusalem would be living in the light of eternity. The process of secularization took centuries. Yet men did finally come to believe that it was possible, provided that one had a privileged insight into history and a proper social and industrial technology, to control and direct the historical process so as to achieve the perfect society on this earth.

American millennialism has never been as violent as the various revolutionary movements of Europe have been—Marxism, for example—but it has remained from the seventeenth century onward a driving and shaping force in our history. One can find it in the essays of Emerson, in the poetry of Walt Whitman, and almost nakedly in Julia Ward Howe's "Battle Hymn of the Republic." It is still a powerful force right down to the present day, though it is now so familiar to most of us that we never refer to it by a term so formidable as millennialism, but speak of it rather fondly as simply the American Dream.

The issue of millennialism is, however, one that sets Faulkner off from a great many other American writers. On this issue, he does not, of course, stand alone. He has companions in American writers like Hawthorne and Melville, and he does not entirely lack companions in the twentieth century. Yet his more old-fashioned notion of history has disquieted and confused many a twentieth-century literary critic, and it sets him off sharply from such twentieth-century writers as Hart Crane and, to mention one whose talents he greatly admired, Thomas Wolfe.

Faulkner is far less visionary than Wolfe, less optimistic, less intoxicated with the greatness of America. By contrast, Faulkner's view is more "Southern" and, though I shall not claim him for Christian orthodoxy, much closer to Saint Augustine's view of history.

Let me recur to the theme of nature once more. Faulkner loves nature: witness the great hymns to nature in "The Bear" and in *The Hamlet*. But he also realizes that man is a fallen creature. Men cannot simply subsist on nature's bounty, living on nuts and fruits and berries, like Milton's Adam, "innocent of fire." Man is a hunter and to some extent a predator. Yet he must respect the thing that he kills and try to be worthy of its death.

When Ike pauses by the grave of Lion and sees again the tin box that contains "Old Ben's dried mutilated paw," he realizes, caught up in his vision of the oneness of nature, that Old Ben is also part of that nature and cries out: "They [the hunters] would give [Ben] his paw back, . . . certainly they would give him his paw back: then . . . no heart to be driven in outrage, no flesh to be mauled and bled." Clearly this outcry expresses a yearning to return to the happy Garden. But it is important to note that in this rhapsodic outburst, the time for returning Ben's paw is almost as remote as eternity itself. The young man is sincere, his vision of harmony and oneness is meaningful, but Ike is not seriously contemplating abstaining from the annual hunt. The last time that we see him in *Go Down, Moses* he is down in the Big Bottom again, with a gun. What does fill him with lasting horror is, not hunting and shedding blood as such, but his vision of the Delta "deswamped and denuded and derivered"—all for the purpose of economic exploitation. The scene that Ike contemplates with horror is one not of man lovingly wedded to nature but of his violent rape of nature.

It must be granted, I think, that if man's veneration for nature is absolute, history becomes impossible. We have the unceasing round of the seasons, birth, copulation, and death, but no proper history. Wild flowers, deer, and squirrels have no "history." Nor do very primitive tribes of human beings. They have instead their creation myths and their often very complex tribal customs and rituals. Even the highly sophisticated Greeks saw human history as a cyclic process rather than a linear succession of events leading to some discernible goal. As for the concept of progress—that could not develop until many centuries later.

Faulkner does have a sense of history—he may even be said to have a providential sense of history. But there is little evidence for assuming that Faulkner believed in automatic progress. It is, in fact, difficult to believe wholeheartedly in progress unless one also believes that man is perfectible. Faulkner doesn't. For him, man is fallible, and Faulkner holds out no hope that he will ever be otherwise. Moreover, Faulkner certainly could not stomach the notion that the perfection of society might be achieved by brainwashing and conditioning its naturally fallible citizens to the point of foolproof docility. One does not have to speculate about what would be Faulkner's answer to B. F. Skinner's argument that mankind can no longer afford freedom but must move to a condition "beyond freedom and dignity." Faulkner prefers a human being who is capable of feats of heroism—even if this means that he will also be capable of acts of sub-bestial cruelty. His fiction is full of instances of both, and of men whose minds and personalities combine great virtue with horrifying vice. Mink Snopes is only one of many such examples.

All of which is to say that Faulkner's view of man is still basically Christian. That is, man stands both inside and outside of nature. He is a natural creature—and must not ever try to repudiate that condition—but also transcends nature and can never be content merely to do what comes naturally. He is condemned to be either worse or better than the other natural creatures. In short, he has a moral and aesthetic life as the wild beast does not, and for him the door into true history is at least ajar.

In part IV of "The Bear," in his impassioned debate with his cousin, Ike is probably speaking for Faulkner when he says of men that God "has created [men] and knew them capable of all things because He had shaped them out of the primal Absolute which contained all and had watched them since in their individual exaltation and baseness." In this same story, Ike again is probably speaking for Faulkner when he says that "human beings always misuse freedom." Man has the freedom to choose, a freedom denied to the other creatures, but inevitably he misuses it and chooses badly. Is the case hopeless, then? Is man utterly doomed? Not wholly, for man—at least according to Ike—can learn through suffering, and in his long colloquy with his cousin he seems to think that a great many of us can learn *only* through suffering.

To many, this will seem to be a somber doctrine, and yet it can also be regarded as optimistic. For the disasters that befall a people need not be totally so, and though history is untidy and horribly wasteful, man's very mistakes may be redeemed—at least in part—in their consequences.

This notion constitutes the very core of Ike's argument that God, in bringing about the defeat of the South in the Civil War, was chastising the land that he really loved and for which he had done so much. Southerners had to learn that slavery was wrong, but they could learn only through suffering, through what was written in blood. Therefore, the defeat of the Southern cause—a defeat that occurred in spite of the valor of the Confederate soldier and the brilliant leadership of people like Lee and Jackson and Forrest—was really a manifestation of God's loving regard.

Cass Edmonds is understandably somewhat shocked by this argument and it will probably never pass muster in a Ph.D. dissertation to be submitted to the history faculty at Columbia or Yale or Harvard. But it does represent a providential view of history, which is all I originally claimed for it. Moreover, whether it is history or just myth, it has its own dignity and perhaps its modicum of truth. It is certainly in the tradition of the Judeo-Christian interpretation of history. I have special reference to the pronouncements of the Old Testament prophets like Isaiah and Jeremiah and in the New Testament to those of Saint Paul. God chastiseth those that he loveth and he does work in mysterious ways, his wonders to perform.

Ike's view of American history is one that is very important for him. It allowed him to preserve his own local loyalties, his pride in family and clan, and his reverence for his own countryside, and yet to feel that the disaster that had befallen his section was not a total or a meaningless disaster. Moreover, it is the easier to hold if you are willing to accept the view that the human being is an inextricable mixture of virtues and vices, of high aspiration, accidental blind spots, and positive sinfulness. Before we leave this matter of Ike's redaction of American history, one or two other points might be made. Ike dismisses the myth of the noble savage. Although admitting the mistakes of the Old World, whose tragic history men properly wanted to escape by finding a new world and a new start, he makes it plain that the Indians who inhabited America were not themselves innocent. Thus, "uncivilized man" is not thereby virtuous, nor can the burden of human history be evaded by shaking the dust of one place from one's feet and setting them down on a new continent.

Some readers have been puzzled by the idealistic Ike McCaslin's bitter attack on the abolitionists who in the Northeast had for a generation and more before the Civil War been thundering against the evils of slavery. They have wondered whether it was not merely perverse local pride that made Ike exult in the valor of the Confederate soldier, whose actions worked against the abolition of slavery, and attack so bitterly the politicians and "men of God" who meant to abolish it.

Local pride is surely involved to some degree, but Ike's case begins to look more plausible if we take into account millennialism. Ike is obviously suspicious of holier-than-thou rhetoric and the self-advertising involved in one's use of it. In particular he hates the abstract violence that he associates with the abolitionist preachers and politicians. By contrast, old John Brown's no-nonsense-about-it direct action to Ike seems admirable. If one means to be violent, then direct action which involves personal risk seems preferable to violent language and high-flown rhetoric which may incite others to violence but leaves the agitator safe. Yet such rhetoric and abstraction are constant features of millennialism. Historically, the millennialist has always claimed to know what causes man to act and what course history is bound to take. We can find such claims made long before millennialists like Auguste Comte and Karl Marx produced their special theories. Faulkner is skeptical of all millennialist claims. He questions whether the abolitionist—or any other millennialist, for that matter—has such a grasp of human psychology or has so cunningly penetrated to the secret springs of history as to be capable of imposing his theoretical solutions upon other people who are actually involved in complicated problems.

The heart of the matter for Faulkner, I am convinced, centers in his revulsion from any abstract theory that somehow contrives to bypass the human situation as encountered by every great artist. So I will now shift terms, from *millennialism,* which points to the goal to be reached, to the term *gnosis,* which has to do with the claim of special knowledge of humanity and history on which the millennialist relies.

In doing so, I lean heavily on the work of Eric Voegelin, who held the Max Weber chair in political science at the University of Munich and was Boyd Professor of Political Science at Louisiana State University. The late Professor Voegelin's magisterial five-volume work is entitled *Order and History.* Voegelin's massive studies in order (social and political) and in history incidentally comment on the origins of Gnosticism in the Hellenistic world and trace the idea down through its several twentieth-century developments. The Gnostic has an overwhelming faith in know-how—in his own know-how, of course—and he seeks to extend his know-how to cover aspects of the human situation that simply cannot be made subject to foolproof prescriptions.

What is the perfect society? Can mankind be organized so perfectly that everybody will be happy? Can men be sufficiently regimented to make that society stable without damage to that which makes them men? The issue is not dead. The average American is at least mildly infected with gnosticism, and bolder and more resolute spirits like B. F. Skinner warn that we will have to give up human dignity and freedom. Professor Skinner thinks that the loss of these is not too much of a price to pay.

Faulkner, of course, would count it far too heavy a price, and though

Faulkner presumably never heard of Voegelin, and might have had great difficulty with Voegelin's terminology, he would have had absolutely no difficulty in grasping his thesis. Indeed, if I am right, he did grasp it independently, coming by it legitimately as a member of a traditional society.

Had Faulkner wanted to tick off gnostic and millennialist pretensions, he could have used an old folk expression which I remember from west Tennessee and probably Faulkner too must have known as a boy in north Mississippi. We used to twit people who held grandiose ideas with expecting to find "salvation in a jug," bottled salvation—on tap, at one's pleasure, just pull the corncob stopper and have a dram. The phrase would constitute an earthy retort to the notion that the human predicament can be resolved by formula and method.

Yet Faulkner, for all his healthy skepticism about recipes for making society healthy, wealthy, and wise, was not a quietist. Specific reforms were necessary. As a man, he spoke out vigorously, sometimes to the annoyance of his friends and neighbors, about conditions that he thought required change. Moreover, as we know, he was unhappy with many aspects of conventional Christianity, particularly as exemplified in some of the more hot-gospeling evangelical sects that he encountered in his native state.

But back to the matter of gnosis. How does it figure in Faulkner's novels? When Uncle Ike's cousin asks him how he knows that God's plan was to set his lowly people free, and how he knows that the Negroes will endure, Ike appeals to the wisdom of the heart, not to mere ratiocination or to laboratory tests. He tells his cousin that "the heart already knows." It is the heart that constitutes the touchstone for the truth about man and his destiny. Again, in *Requiem for a Nun,* when Nancy Mannigoe is having her final interview with the anguished Temple Drake and Temple wants to know how Nancy knows the truth about sin and suffering and hell and heaven, Nancy quite properly says, "I don't know. I believes." No gnosticism here. The great affirmations of ultimate value, even though reasonable men may agree that they are credible, always transcend reason. One cannot "know" them in the sense that he knows a chemical formula. One believes them. They are accepted as a matter of faith.

Faulkner, however, in his novels created at least one gnostic. (I think there are others, but I can mention only one.) He is Thomas Sutpen.

The specific indicia of the gnostic as Voegelin enumerated them are all here. History, for Sutpen, is meaningless and its story of man's limitations and defeats has no message for him. He has complete confidence that he can alter present conditions and reforge his future. But in addition to his admirable confidence and indomitable courage—these are his great virtues—he is truly a gnostic in that he has his own gnosis— that is, his *diagnosis* of human nature and his *prognosis* of history, his blueprint of the future.

Like most such plans, Sutpen's oversimplifies and distorts human nature and history. Mr. Compson is quite correct in applying to Sutpen his homey analogy to cooking: Sutpen believed that the ingredients of morality "were like the ingredients of pie or cake. When once you had measured and balanced them and mixed them and put them into the oven it was all finished and nothing but pie or cake could come out." But such a morality is of course no morality at all: it has become a mechanical formula and the actual nature of the human being is ignored as irrelevant. It is the same insight that forces Mr. Compson to apply the term *innocent* to Sutpen, for if men can do nothing worse than occasionally miscalculate conditions and make mistakes, then the problem of sinfulness has been jettisoned. Sutpen's "innocence" is not virtue but ignorance of the nature of reality. He is no unfallen Adam living in the eye of a loving God, within a paradise of natural beauty and harmony that furnishes him all his wants graciously and without effort on his part. Instead, Sutpen is a kind of superman who assaults the wilderness—today it would be with bulldozer and chain saw—in order to turn the happy Garden into Sutpen's Hundred through an exploit of cold-blooded efficiency—without malice, to be sure, but also without any regret for what he is destroying. Such innocence, as Mr. Compson properly points out, is inhuman and destructive. As the novel suggests, it is also self-destructive.

One last item of the indicia of Voegelin's gnosticism I have already implied: the fanaticism which characterizes the planner who means to execute his "design" come hell or high water, who has no piety with regard to nature and no love for his fellow human beings, and who, when the plan has come a cropper, will admit no more than a mistake of calculation.

In trying to sketch Faulkner's sense of history in contrast to our all-too-familiar American millennialist notions about history, I must not give the impression that Faulkner ever himself becomes doctrinaire or abstract. Rarely, if ever, does he cease to be the artist. He does not force his characters to serve as mouthpieces for his own notions, but lets them speak for themselves. *Absalom, Absalom!* will supply a fine instance of his dramatistic objectivity in this matter. For who are the two young men who work over the evidence in the cold Harvard dormitory and who try to make sense of Sutpen's downfall and of his life and death? One of them, Shreve, is a man who has little sense of history. The past, provided it is a violent past like that of the Old South, is fascinating to him because it seems melodramatic—"It's better than the theater—better than Ben Hur," he exclaims. But the story of Sutpen's family is finally irrelevant to Shreve and, after the game is played out, easy for him to put aside. This is not to say that Shreve is a gnostic. He is simply a young medical student for whom truth is basically laboratory truth, and for whom the most obvious thing about man is the machinery of the human body, which can be scientifically described and which he is now engaged in studying. At any rate, history, as Shreve sees it, holds no terrors to overshadow man's future.

The other member of the pair is obsessed with history. The history of his own region records a lost war and family disasters. The hand of the past rests heavily upon him. Thus, Faulkner has not stacked the cards in favor of what I take to be his own interpretation of history by presenting us with a debate on conceptions of history, with one debater who is quite wrong and serves merely as a foil for the other who is quite right. If Shreve dismisses the past in cavalier fashion, Quentin, having been defeated by it, lets it crush him.

What Faulkner has done, therefore, is to force the reader to find the proper measure of history for himself. Everything in the book is drama. The reader is allowed to watch the various characters try to piece together the few bits of fact that they possess, try to imagine why the characters did and said this or that, and to take part himself in the process of constructing what actually happened and why. But the reader in doing this will necessarily become involved in a second process: that of assessing the degree to which one can ever find the truth in history. I suggest that the sensitive reader will also necessarily become involved in trying to answer a third question: what is the meaning and relevance of history—for himself—and for all men.

Index